Y

ERSITY

L.

CRIMINOLOGY

SAGE RESEARCH PROGRESS SERIES IN CRIMINOLOGY

Published in Cooperation with the American Society of Criminology
Series Editor: **MICHAEL R. GOTTFREDSON,** *State University of New York at Albany*
Founding Series Editor: **JAMES A. INCIARDI,** *University of Delaware*

SAGE RESEARCH PROGRESS SERIES
VOLUME 23

CRIME
SPILLOVER

Edited by
Simon Hakim and
George F. Rengert

Published in cooperation with the
AMERICAN SOCIETY of CRIMINOLOGY

 SAGE PUBLICATIONS   Beverly Hills   London

For information address:

SAGE Publications, Inc.
275 South Beverly Drive
Beverly Hills, California 90212

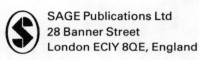

SAGE Publications Ltd
28 Banner Street
London ECIY 8QE, England

Printed in the United States of America

Library of Congress Cataloging in Publication Data

Main entry under title:

Crime spillover.

(Sage research progress series in criminology; v. 23).
"Published in cooperation with the American Society of Criminology."
Contents: Introduction / Simon Hakim and George F. Rengert—Criminal mobility: a review of empirical studies / John P. McIver—Economic theoretical view of criminal spillover / Uriel Speigel—[etc.]
1. Crime and criminals—United States—Addresses, essays, lectures. 2. United States—Administrative and political division—Addresses, essays, lectures.
I. Hakim, Simon. II. Rengert, George F. III. American Society of Criminology. IV. Series.
HV6791.C75   364'.973   81-9285
ISBN 0-8039-1698-1   AACR2
ISBN 0-8039-1699-X (pbk.)

FIRST PRINTING

CONTENTS

TO OUR DAUGHTERS
Liora Hakim
Mireya Rengert

1

Simon Hakim
George F. Rengert
Temple University

INTRODUCTION

The extensive scholarly inquiry into the causes of crime has resulted in an abundance of theoretical explanations for it. Most of these explanations focus on one or more forces acting on the individual to lead him or her into crime. These forces include the dysfunctioning of society, problems in the economy, and innate characteristics of the individual, as well as faults of the victims.

There is less scholarly attention to the actors who commit crimes and who choose between alternatives in that process. It was the recognition that there were few theories with which to interpret criminal choice behavior that led us to this book.

Usually, "opportunities" for crime are measured and described in absolute terms. When the criminal himself or herself is to be considered, the value of "opportunities" becomes more subjective because each criminal has a choice of opportunities within an environment. The criminal selection from and use of that environment is the unifying theme of the chapters that follow. Opportunities in an environment are measured subjectively in terms of who may exploit them, and relatively in terms of other available opportunities.

This relative level of opportunity introduces a spatial and temporal dimension into our reasoning. It entails comparing two or more places or times for committing a crime. The important aspect is how potential criminals evaluate opportunities for crime.

THE ECONOMIC PERSPECTIVE

Economists have long viewed property crime as the result of a rational decision-making process. The economic approach is to consider criminals as planners who consciously are attempting to maximize the monetary and psychic rewards to the criminal act net of all costs. The costs associated with committing a crime include the direct costs involved in planning and implementing the crime, the opportunity costs for lawful activities forfeited in order to commit the criminal act, and the psychic costs associated with the risk of apprehension and punishment. Once criminals are viewed as rational planners, analysis of crime becomes an application of consumer theory which is part of microeconomics.

In order to evaluate the above costs and benefits, the rational criminal must have some criminal opportunities in mind. The question therefore turns not only to whether or not to execute a crime, but also to which opportunity (target) to choose among those available. From an economic perspective, the criminal evaluates the various opportunities possible and chooses the one which is expected to result in the highest net benefit.

The above reasoning outlines one of the most important contributions of economists to understanding criminal behavior—the concept of "utility maximization" by a rational individual evaluating criminal possibilities. It is the traditional economic approach to explain the probability that a person will engage in criminal acts. If we introduce space into the analysis, then the criminal views the net benefits expected of various alternative crime sites. The criminal will choose to execute the crime at that place which yields the highest net returns.

In order to consider the spatial dimension, several "journey to crime" variables enter into the traditional spaceless analysis: explicit transportation costs, set-up costs spent in learning about a less well-known environment, probability of being recognized in a new environment as an outsider, and problems of becoming acquainted with the particular police practices. Spatial choice analysis can be used to describe the criminal evaluation of individual houses or businesses, neighborhoods, city-suburbs, or multijurisdictional metropolitan areas. Once we are dealing with interdependent multijurisdictional environments, economists conceptualize crime occurrences using theoretical crafts they developed to study external effects, another topic in microeconomic theory.

Externalities

While criminals are attempting to maximize their gain by evaluating potential crime locations, communities are attempting to reduce the level of opportunity for criminal gain within their boundaries. This involves costs for community protection which must be balanced against costs which accrue to the community when a criminal act is perpetrated. These latter costs are measured in terms of real property stolen as well as less tangible costs associated with a decrease in the "quality of life" resulting from victimization. There is an incentive on the part of the community to confront crime with a variety of activities. Certain of these activities are designed to reduce the number of individuals who may choose a life of crime. These are termed "crime deterrence" or "corrective measures." They have positive effects on neighboring communities by reducing the number of criminals who might exploit them.

Other measures merely result in making a community less vulnerable to a criminal act relative to its neighboring communities. These are termed "mechanical prevention programs" or "target hardening." Under these circumstances, crime may be displaced to a neighboring community rather than deterred. In other words, it exhibits "negative externalities" for neighboring communities. We will briefly discuss three alternative approaches a community may choose in combating property crimes.

Clearly the most desirable of these activities from a social perspective is an effort to reduce the number of criminals. This effort entails an understanding of criminogenesis. It is usually considered to be monetarily the most costly to the community. Such programs are of a broad social welfare prospective; they require that we cut unemployment, shrink income disparities, and eliminate the social ills of ignorance, racism, and the disintegration of the family. Most such programs permanently increase the criminal's total costs of crime by increasing opportunity costs—the legal earnings. Citizens living in relatively secure sections of our metropolitan areas often feel that the cure is worse than the disease—they characteristically resist the increased taxation and monetary transfers required to wage this type of war on crime. Further, the impacts of such programs on crime reduction are not evident in the short run, and thus are not politically popular.

A second approach to combating crime is to reduce the number of crime occurrences rather than the number of criminals. These programs do not necessarily rechannel the criminal away from a life of crime. Rather, the focus is to reduce criminal activities temporarily by, for example, occupying their time in productive or leisure activities. These activities include educational programs, police athletic groups, and summer work programs for youth in crime-prone neighborhoods. Imprisonment that removes the criminal temporarily from the community could also be included. Two important characteristics of these programs are that they allow less time for crime and, in some cases, less monetary incentive, since legally earned money can substitute, at least partially, for illegal gains.

A final approach to combating crime is to attack it where it occurs; this is termed "hardening an area." These mechanical prevention tactics such as increased police patrols, marking of belongings, and the installation of improved locks deter crime only in cases in which the criminal is not willing to expend the time or effort to exploit the target or to search for another opportunity. This may be the case for young and opportunistic criminals. For the professional criminal however, crime is merely displaced.

Displacement can take on various forms: (1) temporal displacement, when the criminal substitutes another time of the day, week, or season to victimize the same site or area; (2) tactical displacement, when the criminal substitutes a different *modus operandi;* (3) target displacement, when the criminal searches for an easier target in the same area; (4) type of crime displacement, when the criminal substitutes a type of crime not affected by the mechanical tactics of a community; and (5) spatial displacement, when the criminal searches for a new area or region to operate in.

The negative externalities associated with the spatial displacement of crime may be conceptualized as follows. Assuming that a local government optimally allocates resources to harden crime targets, then the benefits to that community from a reduced crime rate net of all costs associated with enforcing the "mechanical measures" and the loss of property due to residual crime will be greater than zero. However, if crimes are being spatially displaced to adjacent communities, then the social benefits (for all locals) net of social costs might be negative. If we assume free flow of resources, then the resources committed to mechanical measures might have higher productivity in alternative uses. Hence, when we consider the entire region, rather than just the initial community, the mechanical prevention activities may be inefficient due to the negative externalities associated with them.

From the criminal's viewpoint, increased police patrolling in a community leads to a higher arrest rate; this lowers a criminal's expected net return in that community whereas the net returns in adjacent communities would remain unchanged. If this results in a relatively high crime payoff in a neighboring community, the economically rational criminal will shift operations into this area. This is the "negative externality" associated with mechanical crime prevention tactics.

Mechanical crime prevention tactics do possess a programmatic advantage. They are easily implemented by local policy makers and reach immediate and measurable results by reducing the local crime rate. Therefore, it is an attractive measure since the efforts are visible to the local constituents and the results can be identified in the short run through the crime statistics. However, the community is protecting itself partially at the expense of neighboring communities.

In reality it is difficult to classify all public anticrime activities into the broad categories of "corrective" and "mechanical" measures. A particular measure by police may have the effect of both reducing the number of crimes (corrective) and of displacing some crimes (mechanical), depending on the attributes of the affected criminal population, the type of crime considered, and related environmental factors. For example, increased police patrolling in Community A might deter young opportunistic burglars who act on the "spur of the moment" when a good opportunity arises. However, the same police activity may change the location of the crime to Community B for the older professional burglar who plans criminal activities more carefully.

Problems and Prospects
for the Economic Perspective

The economic model of the rational criminal provides an important dimension for understanding unlawful activities in our society. If indeed a criminal is rational and behaves similarly to the consumer, then we can apply the well-grounded theories developed in microeconomics to this area. Hence, the cause-effect relationship that microeconomic theory implies is important in order to explain criminal behavior, to predict future crime levels, and to suggest effective law enforcement policies.

These models are not without shortcomings, however. One of the most serious shortcomings is the assumption that all property criminals are alike — economically rational individuals. Greater insight might result if we treat separately the categories of criminals defined by demographic and economic characteristics, mode of transportation, criminal expertise, degree of risk aversion, and type of crime practiced. Many of these topics are a central focus of more general criminological studies. Economic analysis could benefit from a greater degree of integration of findings contained in these studies.

A second shortcoming of the economic perspective is the assumption that each component of the utility maximization model has equal weight. Investigations to determine relative weights to be assigned to different cost and benefit factors clearly are needed. Again, consideration of criminological findings in this regard could be used to improve economic models. Furthermore, we might consider separate models to explain the number of criminals, the number of crimes, and criminal displacement, since different prevention tactics apply to each.

Finally, we must consider the role of regional cooperation in crime control. Target hardening may be economically efficient when it is shared by all communities, that is, it may deter crimes while maintaining net social benefits. It may be least effective when communities operate on a competitive independent basis to make themselves less vulnerable than their neighbors. In other words, cooperative efforts may reduce crime if they make the time, effort, or cost of crime greater than the criminal is willing to spend to attain illegal gains. As yet, we know little about the relative merits of public cooperation versus competition in crime control.

It should be stressed that even cooperative efforts which extend to the whole metropolitan area and which strive to minimize the net social cost of crime are not likely to reduce crime to zero. A certain level of crime is socially acceptable where the total costs needed to eliminate it are higher than the benefits resulting from its elimination.

TYPOLOGY OF CRIMINAL SPATIAL BEHAVIOR

The geographic perspective provides a typology of criminal spatial movement that follows closely demographic concepts used in human migration studies. "Criminal spatial mobility" is the spatial movement necessary to commit most property crimes. There are characteristic distances associated with specific crimes and characteristic distances associated with the site-specific transportation facilities available to the criminal population. Movement over space entails costs of time and money, but is necessary in order to exploit the subjectively identified "best targets." In other words, in order to maximize economic gain, the criminal chooses among sites located at different distances from the origin area.

If a political boundary is crossed in the journey from the origin of the criminal to the crime site, we term this movement interjurisdictional "crime spillover." Assuming, again, economically rational behavior of the criminal, interjurisdictional movement could be caused by a change in an equilibrium condition in which the net benefits of crime in the origin community falls relative to the net benefits in adjacent communities. This change would result in an incentive for the criminal to travel to an adjacent community to commit crime. Such travel is considered to be crime spilling over from the origin community to an adjacent community.

Interjurisdictional "crime displacement" is a special case of crime spillover in which the criminal is attempting to avoid an increased certainty of punishment caused by public and/or private expenditure of funds on mechanical programs. These mechanical programs include police patrols, police education programs to teach citizens to secure property, citizen patrols, and improved security systems, lighting, and similar devices which would increase the risk of apprehension and/or assist in producing better evidence to the courts such that the probability of being punished by the courts increases. The rational criminal is "pushed" out of the community by increased relative certainty of punishment and attracted to a neighboring community which is more appealing.

Crime displacement is a special case of crime spillover. Crime can spill over from Community A to Community B as a result of increased wealth, which indicates higher returns to burglaries at B, or more police activities in Community A. However, crime is displaced from A to B only as a result of the increased police activity. In other words, displacement is the "push" out of Community A rather than the "pull" into Community B.

MEASUREMENT PROBLEMS AND POLICY CONSIDERATIONS

To analyze crime spillover, data on criminals who change the locations of their operations to other communities are needed. Information on their socioeconomic and demographic characteristics, their gain from criminal activity, and most importantly, their motives for shifting their operations is needed. This information can only come from interviews with criminals; however, only a small subsample of the total criminal population—those arrested and convicted of an offense—are available. Rates of arrest and conviction in most metropolitan areas are very low and the small sample of apprehended and convicted offenders may not well represent the profile and motives of the whole mobile criminal population. Therefore, an unknown bias may exist in much of the data based on convicted individuals.

Another problem is one of data availability at a scale necessary for most microeconomic analysis. Interview data is very costly to gather and access to criminals is often regulated by laws and justice officials. Because of these problems, most empirical studies use indirect data such as attributes of communities as a whole rather than of the actual criminal population and their associated motives for crime. For example, the median value of housing is used to indicate the expected return to residential burglary in that community. Cross-sectional population profiles drawn from the Census of Population are substituted for the actual characteristics of criminals from a community. Police expenditures and police patrols per capita are used to measure costs to criminals. Any of these surrogate measures can introduce unknown biases in results.

Motives for criminal behavior are very difficult to detect from aggregate data but are important to an understanding of the crime displacement phenomenon. Since the cause of crime displacement (target hardening by mechanical measures) is relatively easy to institute and demonstrates immediate results to local constituents, it is an attractive measure for the *local* policy makers. However, the regional or metropolitan level crime may not have changed if criminals simply avoid the original target area and increase their activities in surrounding communities. The net benefits to the region are unclear, and may be negative when one considers the cost of implementing the target hardening programs, thus the local community gains at the neighbor's expense. For this reason, spatial crime displacement is important to recognize and to include in regional planning policies.

Below are some examples of regional policies that have been advocated in order to address the problem of crime displacement.

(1) Consolidate all or some police functions across jurisdictions in order to internalize the external effects of crime displacement.
(2) Pressure crime "exporting" localities (perhaps through a taxing scheme) to shift resources from "mechanical" to "corrective" prevention programs.
(3) Subsidize corrective programs in exporting localities from funds collected in crime importing localities in order to reduce the criminal population.
(4) Improve interjurisdictional voluntary cooperation in order to combat the mobile criminal.
(5) Encourage localities to spend more on "corrective" rather than "mechanical" programs by offering matching funds provided by federal and state governments.

These are but a few of the strategies that address the problem of an increasingly mobile criminal population. They are not trivial solutions; they gain importance with an increasingly mobile criminal population operating within an economically, socially, and ethnically integrated metropolitan area composed of fragmented political systems.

SCOPE OF THE BOOK

This book introduces the reader to current research focused on criminal spatial mobility with an emphasis on crime spillover as viewed from an economic perspective. The contributors to this volume are among those scholars who wrote the seminal works on this topic and have been most active in building the present state of our knowledge. The chapters were selected from among the invited works presented at two special sessions and a workshop chaired by the editors of this volume at the 1980 Meetings of the American Society of Criminology, and other manuscripts invited from those who could not attend the meetings.

We have not intended to present a one-sided perspective. Indeed, the reader will note that there still is not general agreement on whether or not crime displacement exists in a significant form, and if so, its significance for policy consideration. It should be noted that the following analysis of interjurisdictional crime spillover uses aggregative data which do not allow us to consider carefully the decision-making process of the individual criminal. In other words, we do not know how the various components of the criminal's environment are weighed at the individual level. In economic terms, we do not know what the criminal's utility function is. It is our hope that these works will prove seminal to further in-depth analysis of criminal spatial movement.

Chapter 2, by John McIver, sets the stage for the subsequent analyses by providing a general overview of criminal mobility, crime spillover, and the policy implications of these criminal movement patterns. His discussion of the relationship between public policies and deterred crime which results from these efforts at crime control is especially timely. It points up the difficulty in measuring something that never takes place—deterred crime.

This work is followed by two short theoretical works. The first, by Uriel Spiegel, illustrates the existence of an equilibrium in public expenditure for crime control by adjacent localities in the presence of crime spillover and interjurisdictional competition in crime control. The amount spent by all localities on security proves to be nonoptimal. A better resource allocation can be reached by interjurisdictional cooperation rather than competition. John Sorrentino places the problem of crime spillover into a welfare economic perspective which focuses on the problem of economic externalities associated with public expenditures for crime control.

The next four chapters are empirical studies. Stephen Mehay expands his earlier seminal work by incorporating "profitability" of crime with the risk of arrest to determine incentives for crime displacement in Los Angeles. He concludes that police consolidation will have little effect on the magnitude of crime displacement. Lee McPheters and William Stronge argue that previous studies may have misspecified the law enforcement activity variable in their estimating equations. They argue that when law enforcement activity is considered in absolute rather than relative terms, crime displacement effects are negligible in the Boston area. Richard Fabrikant examines the actual movement of juvenile delinquents in Los Angeles and concludes that these criminals are sensitive to areal variations in wealth and law enforcement effort. Martin Katzman demonstrates the importance of relative location (crime potential) to a criminal population in determining the victimization of a community. His analysis highlights the importance of spatial movement of criminals by demonstrating that the characteristics of surrounding communities are as important a consideration as the characteristics of a local population in determining the local crime rate. Finally, Daryl Hellman synthesizes the work of the above authors. She notes that there are few firm conclusions that can be drawn to date. She points to the need for more comprehensive studies, which should consider other components of the criminal justice system besides the police.

We are just beginning to tap the vast amount of information required to truly understand the criminal decision-making process, criminal spatial mobility, and public policy alternatives. At this time, studies focusing on individual criminals and how they weigh spatial alternatives are especially needed. This volume is a beginning. It is our hope that a renewed interdisciplinary research thrust will carry us further toward answers to the many vexing problems that remain.

2

John P. McIver

Indiana University—Bloomington

CRIMINAL MOBILITY
A Review of Empirical Studies

Human beings are mobile creatures. This basic fact is the focus of an expanding criminal justice literature. Criminals, potential victims, and the police move along social and spatial dimensions, each seeking some advantage over one or more of the other groups. Offenders seek out undefended individuals or unguarded positions. Potential victims participate in daily activities. Some, however, move more cautiously than others, cognizant of the dangers created by their movements to and from particular locations. Police attempt to defend both individuals and desirable positions. Because they are unable to defend all positions at all times, police movement is predicated on providing some protection to all targets in order to minimize their attractiveness to criminals.

This swirl of activity creates uncertainty for all of these actors. Criminals do not know when and where the police will appear. Targets that seem ripe one minute will turn sour the next with the arrival of a patrol car. Potential victims, likewise, have little idea where their protection is currently located or where they are most vulnerable. Victim mobility offers the criminal a choice of opportunities. The offender can wait to commit a crime until the victim moves from a defended to an undefended position. Even better, the criminal can rely on an individual's lack of information and wait for the victim to come into his territory (the "spider's lair" theory of mugging). The availability of choice makes police defense of citizens and their property all the more difficult.

This chapter focuses on the current empirical literature on criminal mobility. The work of criminologists, urban geographers, and economists outlining the extent of criminal mobility is discussed first. Then, three related topics are discussed. First, what factors have we discovered that reduce, facilitate, redirect, or otherwise cause criminal movement. Second, do social scientists all use the same terminology to describe this phenomena? Third, can policy recommendations be identified that would either help police deal with the mobile criminal or provide citizens with ways to improve personal safety?

LITERATURE REVIEW

In 1973, the National Advisory Commission on Criminal Justice Standards and Goals announced:

> Criminal activity is often multijurisdictional. The success of each police agency in its operations has a direct effect on criminal activity in neighboring jurisdictions.

Several assumptions underlie the commission's statements:

> Criminals are mobile.
>
> Criminals are mobile beyond jurisdictional lines. This might be because jurisdictional lines are not salient to criminal eyes. Alternatively, criminals may recognize advantages in crossing jurisdiction boundaries.
>
> Police operations in one jurisdiction affect the level of crime in another. This assumption implies that police operations are effective locally.

Consider first the question of whether criminals are mobile. Then consider the logical extention of this question;

whether jurisdictional boundaries are crossed in criminal activity. The answers provided by contemporary research are presented in Table 2.1. The findings contained in these eight studies, as they pertain to our concerns, are as follows:

> While criminals are mobile, they don't seem to go very far in committing a crime. A majority of crimes appear to take place within a mile of the criminal's residence. This conclusion seems true for all types of crime. Violence may be more prevalent a little closer to home, but burglars either don't own their own cars, can't afford taxis, or most likely, prefer to work known territory.

> Nothing is known about travel between jurisdictions. This question has not been discussed in the literature. The closest thing available to an answer to the question posed above is the map provided by Capone and Nichols (1976), that shows the movement of all robbery trips within the Miami SMSA. It is obvious that jurisdictional boundaries are crossed to commit some of the crimes, but the number is not reported.

While these studies of criminal movement tell us little about the movement of criminals from one jurisdiction to others, they do not rule out such movement. In fragmented metropolitan areas in particular, very little distance must be travelled before the criminal is out of his or her home community and into the next. Additionally, the methods used in most of these studies are probably biased against the interjurisdictional criminal. Data were gathered by interviewing adjudicated (that is, caught) criminals. If we assume that the interjurisdictional criminal is more professional, he or she is at least likely to be caught consequently less likely to be interviewed.

When we consider what factors limit criminal mobility, knowledge of the territory and opportunity are probably the principal limiting conditions. Criminal actions are based on information about victim behavior patterns, the potential rewards, and protective features of the crime site. Usually, this information is more available for areas near the offender's residence. Opportunities limit mobility in the sense that they tend to exist in abundance. There is often little need for the criminal to acquire information about the opportunity structure of distant places.

Let us turn to the final assumption: Police activity affects criminal behavior. Many of the principal nonexperimental, cross-sectional investigations of the reduction of crime rates by increased sanctions are presented in Table 2.2. (For a more comprehensive overview of this literature, see Chaiken, 1976; Greenberg, 1977; or Blumstein et al., 1978.) It is obvious that the conclusions drawn by each author are the result of the sample analyzed, the operationalization of crime rates and sanctioning rates, and the statistical technique used in estimating the impact of sanctions on crime. The weight of the recent evidence (with the exception of Forst, 1976) appears to support the following conclusions:

> Police efforts reduce crime rates. (The magnitude of this relationship is unknown and is not considered large.)

> Increases in the crime rate result in increases in police effort.

As there is little consensus among researchers as to what constitutes a properly specified and operationalized model of the supply of crime and the sanctioning effect, these conclusions must remain very tentative.

Table 2.3 contains a summary of a number of analyses that explicitly treat time as an important factor in the relationship between criminal and anticriminal actions. Again, the findings of each study seem to vary with the choice of data, operationalization, and statistical methodology. Votey and Phillips (1974) and Land and Felson (1976) find that sanctions reduce crime while Jones (1973), Logan (1975), and Greenberg et al. (1979) find that sanctions have little effect on levels of crime. None of these analyses report a positive relationship between crime and law enforcement activity, an initially counter-intuitive result of many of the early cross-sectional efforts. Again, Table 2.3 suggests the conclusion that police and prosecutorial activity may have some, but not much, impact on crime.

(text continues on page 28)

TABLE 2.1 A Summary of Empirical Studies of Criminal Mobility

Author	Location and Date of Study	Type of Criminal Activity (Number of Cases)	Principal Findings	
White (1932)	Indianapolis 1930	felonies (personal and property) (N = 638)	Crime	Mean Distance to Criminal's Residence
			Rape	1.52 miles
			Assault	0.91
			Manslaughter	0.11
			Auto theft	3.43
			Embezzlement	2.79
			Robbery	2.14
			Burglary	1.76
			Grand larceny	1.53
			Petit larceny	1.42
Bullock (1955)	Houston 1945–1949	homicides (N = 489)	57% occur within 0.4 miles of assailant's residence.	
Normandeau (1968)	Philadelphia	robbery	Mean distance traveled is 1.57 miles.	
Turner (1969)	Philadelphia 1960	juvenile delinquency: assault and vandalism (N = 502)	Mean distance traveled is 0.4 miles. 75% occur within 1 mile of juvenile's residence; range is 0–23 miles.	

Study	Location	Crime	Findings
Amir (1971)	Philadelphia 1958, 1960	rape (N = 885)	72% occur within 5 city blocks of the rapist's residence.
Reppetto (1976)	Boston and a second medium-sized city	robbery burglary (N = 245)	Robbery: mean distance traveled is 0.6 miles; 90% occur within 1.5 miles. Burglary: mean distance is 0.5 miles; 93% occur within 1.5 miles.
Capone and Nichols (1976)	Miami SMSA 1971	Robbery (N = 825)	Armed robbery: 23% occur within 1 mile; 59% within 3 miles. Unarmed robbery: 36% occur within 1 mile; 75% within 3 miles.
Pope (1980)	selected areas in 6 California jurisdictions: San Francisco, Oakland, Los Angeles, San Diego, Los Angeles County, Orange County 1972	burglary (N = 1196)	52% occur within 1 mile of burglar's residence.

TABLE 2.2 Cross-Sectional Studies of Police Deterrence of Criminal Activities

Author	Sample	Independent Variable	Dependent Variable	Estimation Technique	Findings
Morris and Tweeten (1971)	754 cities (1967, 1968)	police per capita	violent crime property crime	OLS	Crime increased with additional police for all cities but those over 1 million population.
Greenwood and Wadycki (1973)	212 SMSAs (1960)	police per capita	violent crime property crime	3SLS	Crime increased with additional police. The violent crime rate increases more rapidly than property crime rate as police manpower increases.
Ehrlich (1973)	47 states (1940, 1950, 1960)	probability of imprisonment average prison term	violent crime property crime	OLS 2SLS	Crime decreased with additional expenditure for police services. The effect is similar for property and violent crimes.
Tittle and Rowe (1974)	Florida: 67 counties, 178 cities (1971)	probability of arrest	felony offenses	correlation, scatter-plots, partial correlation	Crime rates are negatively related to clearance rates. A threshold effect is noted for probabilities of arrest greater than 0.3.

Study	Sample	Variables	Crime type	Method	Findings
McPheters and Stronge (1974)	43 larger U.S. cities (1970)	police expenditure per capita	felony offenses	OLS with lagged crime rate	Crime rates are reduced by increased police expenditure.
Swimmer (1974)	all cities 100,000 + (1960)	police expenditure per capita	violent crime property crime	OLS 2SLS	OLS—crime increases (insignificantly) with additional expenditure for police services. 2SLS—crime decreases (insignificantly) with additional expenditure for police services.
Pogue (1975)	66 SMSAs (1968)	clearance rates police expenditure per capita	felony offenses	2SLS	Crime decreases as clearance rates increase. However, police expenditures have no effect on clearance rates.
Forst (1976)	50 states (1970)	probability of incarceration average prison term	felony offenses	2SLS	Crime is not affected by the probability or severity of punishment. However, the probability of punishment is reduced as crime increases.

While the research reviewed in Tables 2.2 and 2.3 is based on analyses of aggregate police and crime statistics, a third approach to the study of deterrence has focused on local, programmatic efforts to reduce crime. A limited experimental methodology has been used to assess the impact of changes in police operational tactics in a number of cities and counties. The results of these attempts are condensed in Table 2.4.

These quasi-experimental studies were designed principally to assess reduction in crime rates after the intervention of a new anticrime strategy. In most of the cases reviewed here, this "new strategy" simply required increases in the number of police officers on the street. The evaluation of this strategy then involved ascertainment of whether or not crimes were reduced. The Kansas City Preventive Patrol Experiment attempted to demonstrate the differential productivity of alternative patterns of patrol, while the Hartford Neighborhood Redevelopment Project illustrates the coproduction of safety by police, citizens, and neighborhood planners.

The results of all of these projects indicate that police can have an impact on crime if manpower levels are high enough to constitute a visible sanction.[1] In most cases, crime rates were reduced with large increases in police manpower. Where increased personnel did not affect crime rates, it is likely no change occurred because the manpower increases did not change the actual sanction levels; for example, the increase in county police personnel reported by Knapp et al. (1980) has the effect of reducing response time to approximately 16 minutes, an interval that the Kansas City Response Time Experiment (Kansas City Police Department, 1978) demonstrated was far too long to have any impact on arrest rates. Similar criticisms have been made of the Kansas City Preventive Patrol Experiment (Larson, 1975).

Several of these projects did recognize that police might have some impact on criminal activity other than reducing it. In particular, they suggest that criminals might, in response to increased police pressure, move to other locations to commit crimes, commit crimes at other times,

(text continues p. 32)

TABLE 2.3 Aggregate Time Series and Panel Studies of Police Deterrence of Criminal Activities

Author	Sample	Independent Variable	Dependent Variable	Estimation Technique	Findings
Jones (1973)	155 cities (1958–1970)	one year change in police manpower police expenditure	one year change in UCR crimes	correlations	Year to year changes in police manpower and expenditures are not related to changes in the crime rate. This conclusion holds after controls for population, population change, income, and governmental structure.
Votey and Phillips (1974)	national (1953–1968; N = 16)	larceny/ clearance ratio	larceny rate	2SLS	Crime rates are negatively related to clearance rates which are a function of expenditure for police service.
Logan (1975)	50 states (1964–1968)	arrest rate	index crime rate	2-wave cross-lagged panel model	Both the contemporaneous and the lagged effects of arrest rates on crime rates were approximately zero.
Land and Felson (1976)	national (1947–1972; N = 26)	police expenditure per capita	property crime rate violent crime rate	OLS	Both property crime rates and violent crime rates are reduced by increased police expenditure even when lagged crime rates are included as independent variables.
Greenberg et al. (1979)	98 U.S. cities with populations greater than 25,000 (1964–1970)	clearance rate	index crime rate	3-wave cross-lagged panel model: LISREL estimates	Arrest rates have no significant impact on crime rates whether one examines contemporaneous or lagged relationships.

TABLE 2.4 Quasi-Experimental Studies of Police Deterrence (Reduction and Displacement)

Author	Location	Deterrence Program	Findings
Press (1971)	New York City	40% manpower increase in the 20th Precinct, October 1966; data: 1963-1967	Certain crimes decreased with manpower increase; 5% decrease in "inside" felonies; 36% decrease in "outside" felonies; misdemeanors not affected significantly. The major displacement effect was observed in Central Park, which experienced an increase in felonies of ⅓ the decrease in the 20th Precinct. (However, police manpower in Central Park decreased 11% during the period of the study.)
Kelling et al. (1974)	Kansas City	comparison of reactive vs. proactive patrol strategies; 1971	No effect on crime rate as measured by index crimes and victimization surveys. No spillover effect was observed, with the possible exception of auto theft.
Chaiken et al. (1974)	New York City	245% increase in subway police in 1965; data: 1963-1970	Both felonies and misdemeanors on the subways were reduced as were token booth robberies for 2 years, after which crime rates returned to preintervention levels. (Problem with data corruption, however; see Chaiken, 1976.) Slight time displacement was observed. Location displacement was possible in the increase in bus robberies in 1969.
Wilson (1975)	New York City	manpower doubled in the 25th Precinct; 1955	Part 1 crimes decreased substantially—55%. However, reported part 2 crimes—gambling, prostitution, etc.—increased 140%. No attempt was made to measure displacement effects.
Dahmann (1975)	Denver Cleveland St. Louis	additional police added to targeted high-crime neighborhoods; 1972-1973	Outside crimes in target areas were reduced relative to unaffected areas. No strong displacement was found in adjacent neighborhoods.

Schnelle et al. (1975)	Nashville	I. home-burglary saturation patrol II. police walking patrol	I. No significant change in burglaries in targeted areas; no significant change during other shifts or in control areas. II. Reported crime increased in both police zones in which foot officers were available to the public.
Schnelle et al. (1977)	Nashville	saturation patrolling patrol movement increased 400%; 1976	Part 1 crimes decreased, but only for night shifts; no decrease was observed for the day shifts. No surrounding zone experienced any significant change in Part 1 crimes. Nor was there any change in the crime rate on shifts during which the saturation patrol did not operate.
Hartford Institute of Criminal and Social Justice (1979)	Hartford (Asylum Hill Neighborhood Development)	redesign of a neighborhood to reduce vulnerability to crime combined with special neighborhood police team; 1976-1977	Burglary decreased 42%; street robbery decreased 27.5%. (These reductions were verified by victimization surveys.) No displacement of burglaries but possible movement of street robbery. Arrests rose significantly.
Knapp et al. (1980)	Lexington County, South Carolina	37% increase in patrol personnel; February and May, 1977	No evidence of change in the county crime rate for violent or property crimes after the personnel increase. Average response time decreased from 17.44 minutes to 15.82 minutes (9.3%).

when the police presence is less intense, or change their preferred crime to one less susceptible to police attention. Several studies examined one or more possible types of crime displacement. Very few spillovers were observed. Press (1971), for example, suggests the increase of crime in an area (Central Park) bordering the study neighborhood (20th Precinct) where police effort was increased might be due to the displacement of criminal activity. Unfortunately, Central Park experienced an 11 percent officer decrease during the study period. Increases in the Central Park crime rate, therefore, might be due to Central Park police effort, the export of crime by police effort in the 20th Precinct, criminals' perception of relative police effort in these two areas, or simply an exogenous effect such as a change in victim behavior during the study period. Kelling et al. (1974), Chaiken et al. (1974), and the Hartford Institute of Criminal and Social Justice (1979) all report possible displacement of criminal activity. None of these studies, however, offer unqualified evidence that criminal activities have changed locations or that police practices are responsible for the alteration of offender behavior. Dahmann (1975), Schnelle et al. (1975), and Schnelle et al. (1977) report no shifts in the location or target of criminal acts after police manpower levels are altered.

Given the literature on criminal movement and general deterrence, these findings seem reasonable. Major spillovers do not occur because criminals prefer to operate in known territory. Furthermore, detecting small changes in crime due to police activities may be impossible given limited funding for experimental programs, limited duration of those programs, and limited control over "control" neighborhoods.

Most of the simultaneous equation examinations of the relationship between crime and law enforcement have not considered the displacement of crime because researchers have been too busy trying to establish empirical support for the hypothesized relationships between these two variables, that is, crime should have a positive impact on police activities, while police activities should have a negative impact on crime. Recently, however, the possibility that crime is displaced rather than reduced by law enforcement sanctions has received some attention. This literature is presented in Table 2.5.

Each of these four studies identified statistically significant displacement of crime from one area to another and attributed this movement to differential sanctioning levels between communities. Mehay (1977) finds that crime rates are statistically related to intercommunity differences in police manpower. Increases in local manpower increase the crime rates in neighboring jurisdictions. Police are effective only in exporting offenders who commit property crimes (including robbery). Individuals who engage in violent crimes, he argues, are not affected by or cognizant of relative police effort. Focusing on index crimes, Deutsch et al. (1979) also identify the displacement of crime by police effort. They find, contrary to the expectations of many, that crime is displaced from the suburbs to the central city rather than from the central city of Atlanta to its suburbs. Fabrikant (1979), with access to police records for adjudicated juvenile offenders, is able to analyze the actual movement of juvenile offenders rather than infer movement from differential crime rates. He finds that different arrest rates clearly affect the location of juvenile robberies. Sanctioning, however, does not have an impact on the location of other juvenile property crimes.

Hakim et al. (1979) synthesize the cross-sectional models of deterrence and displacement. They simultaneously demonstrate the reduction of crime by local police effort (operationalized as police expenditures per capita) and the displacement of crime into a jurisdiction by increased police efforts elsewhere. Statistically significant spillovers exist for auto thefts and residential burglaries, but larceny rates are not affected by the crime-fighting efforts of other communities. The authors replicate Mehay's (1977) finding that police do not cause violent crime to be displaced from one community to its neighbor.

TABLE 2.5 Nonexperimental Studies of Police Displacement of Criminals

Author	Location	Independent Variable	Dependent Variable	Estimation Technique	Findings
Mehay (1977)	46 cities in Los Angeles Metropolitan Area (1969)	difference in patrol officers per capita between a jurisdiction and its neighbors	violent crime rates property crime rates	OLS	Significant displacement of property crimes occurs. A 10% increase in differential police effort causes a 1% rise in crime in each adjacent community. For this increase in police effort about one third of the property crimes deterred are exported. There is no displacement of violent crimes.
Deutsch et al. (1979)	Atlanta (1974)	average manpower and interzone distances	criminal movement	Network flow analysis	No displacement of criminals from inner city to suburb occurs; significant displacement of criminals from suburb to inner city is observed.

Fabrikant (1979)	Los Angeles (1972-1973)	relative clearance ratios among LA police districts	property crime rates	OLS	Juvenile behavior is reactive to clearance ratios in different sections of Los Angeles for robbery, but not for burglary and larceny. The percentage of offenses occurring outside the district in which the juvenile resides ranges from 60% to 6% for robberies, 48% to 6% for burglaries, and 61% to 10% for larcencies. Spillovers increase with increased economic opportunity and decrease as distance to targets increase.
Hakim et al. (1979)	94 New Jersey suburban communities (1970)	police expenditures per capita weighted average of police expenditures per capita in neighboring communities	property crime rates	2SLS	Property crime increases with increased police expenditures in neighboring communities. Local police expenditures, however, reduce property crime in the community. The impact of local police expenditures on the local crime rate is greater than the effect of expenditures for police services by neighboring communities.

Each of these four studies of crime displacement finds some impact of police effort in neighboring communities on the local crime rate. Differential policing, however, only seems to affect property crimes. Despite the statements by adjudicated criminals that they do not concern themselves with police actions (Goodman et al., 1966; Conklin, 1972; Repetto, 1974), criminals appear to behave as if they were aware of the relative probabilities of detection and capture.[2] Crimes of passion, on the other hand, are not affected by the activities of police in diverse jurisdictions.

While the studies summarized in Tables 2.1 through 2.5 are in no way exhaustive, they are meant to be representative of the research efforts to date. The empirical results just reviewed with respect to criminal mobility and police deterrence and displacement of crime must be considered tentative. Criminals do appear to be mobile although we do not know the extent to which they cross jurisdictional boundaries. Police effort does appear to reduce crime although it appears likely that environmental and demographic characteristics of offenders, victims, and settings are critical variables affecting the incidence of crime. Displacement of crime by police activity is limited, but then few of these research projects were explicitly designed to study such consequences of law enforcement activity.

CRIMINAL MOBILITY— AN ECONOMIC PERSPECTIVE

Economists (Table 2.5) have approached the study of criminal movement from the general perspective of public goods theory. Public goods are those available to all individuals simultaneously (Samuelson, 1954, 1955). Such goods are defined in terms of two principal characteristics. First, the consumption by one individual does not decrease the consumption by another. This condition is known as non-subtractibility or jointness of supply. Second, the exclusion of potential consumers of this type of good is not feasible.

Police services have regularly been treated as public goods (for an exception, see Weicher, 1971). While certain aspects of policing do not exhibit jointness of supply (for example, congestion effects occur during high demand periods) and exclusion is sometimes feasible (for example, certain potential clientele can be ignored), the concern here is with the deterrence (reduction and displacement) of crime. To the extent that potential criminals decide not to commit crimes or decide to commit them in other communities, police can be said to provide a local public good for the citizens residing within their jurisdictions. All citizens are safer if the potential criminal gives up his trade or goes elsewhere. Exclusion of citizens from this increased safety is difficult if not impossible.

When the well-being of one community is affected by the production of law enforcement in another, an external effect or production externality has occurred (Buchanan and Stubblebine, 1962). If the welfare of the first community increases, it is experiencing a positive external effect of the activities within the second community. If the first community's welfare decreases, it is suffering from a negative externality.

The crime-fighting effort by police agencies has two basic goals — deterring the criminal from committing a crime and apprehending him or her once the crime has been committed. Under certain conditions, successful pursuit of these goals in a politically fragmented metropolitan area is both difficult to achieve and hard to finance.

If criminals are mobile and react to police effort, then external effects may occur with production of police services. Apprehension of criminals in one jurisdiction obviously eliminates them as threats to a neighboring jurisdiction. Thus, positive benefits accrue to these neighboring communities who have not paid for this police service. Deterrence may have two external effects. Police effort may convince the potential criminal that it is unprofitable to commit an unlawful act. If this individual decides that the probability of success elsewhere is not greater, or feels that the transportation costs offset the gains from crime, then this person has been effectively eliminated from the class of criminals. This effect, together with the removal of criminals from circulation by apprehension can be termed the *"global deterrence"* effect of police activity. Since many potential criminals could have committed crimes in neighboring jurisdictions, their elimination is a positive benefit for which these communities have not paid.

Deterrence, however, can have a second impact on crime. Rather than remove the criminal from circulation, the effectiveness of local law enforcement may cause the criminal to go "next door" to prey on a (relatively) unprotected community. This latter phenomenon is known as a displacement effect. Displacement of crime is the externality of law enforcement, that is, the movement of an offender from one jurisdiction to another *as a consequence of police activity.* Citizens in one community are forced to bear a reduction in their safety because of the law enforcement practices in adjacent communities.[3]

Our discussion, then, suggests two types of police activities devoted to the reduction of metropolitan crime; one is a public "good," and the other is a public "bad." Empirical studies have tended to focus only on the latter effect—the displacement of crime. The external effects of law enforcement are a *sum* of the *absolute* values of these positive and negative benefits.[4]

The study of externalities is particularly frustrating because the primary focus of analysis is an unobservable quantity. In cross-sectional analyses, the presence of external effects due to police and prosecutorial activities are estimated from differences in observed crime rates between jurisdictions (after appropriate controls for local factors affecting the supply of crime). Yet, this is not a completely satisfactory method. First, this procedure obscures the magnitude of external effects by failing to distinguish deterred crime (a positive externality) from displaced crime (a negative externality). Second, the procedure obscures the magnitude of external effects because observed crime rates rather than victimization rates are the subject of these studies. Third, there are known differences among police department reporting practices that would probably lead to biased estimates of aggregate external effects. In particular, many county and state police departments, acting as overlapping agencies, may maintain records services for small police departments. These overlapping agencies do not necessarily credit the smaller departments on their crime reports to the Department of Justice.

In contrast to the economic focus on externalities, urban geographers and many criminologists are more concerned about where criminals operate, and why they operate in such locations. Obviously, the question "why?" permits the answer "because of the police," but by and large the focus is on personal economic and sociological reasons for criminal mobility. For example, the relative attractiveness of targets may be one causal factor underlying the movement of offenders.[5] The "why?" questions of the urban geographer and criminologist can easily be subsumed within an economic model of the supply of crime and the demand for protection. The important distinction between these various perspectives, however, is in their perception of what type of criminal mobility should be the focus of examination. These differences are discussed next.

THE COMPONENTS OF CRIME RATE

The varied meanings of criminal mobility may be more precisely stated with the help of several simple equations denoting some of the conceptual components of crime rates. First, let us define the observed (reported) crime rate within an isolated community as the "true" crime rate minus the crimes deterred by the police.[6] In symbolic form:

$$OLC_i = TLC_i - DC_i \qquad [1]$$

where: OLC_i is the observed crime rate of community i;
TLC_i is the true crime rate of community i; and
DC_i is the crime deterred by the police force serving community i.

"True local crime" is a concept that may cause some consternation. Yet, as the term is used here, it is consistent with the deterrence and supply of crime literature of the last two decades. TLC_i is the level of crime that exists in a community in the absence of sanctions for unlawful behavior. It is, if one takes the deterrence literature as a point of view, an intercept construct—the level of crime occurring at police/prosecutorial activity levels of zero. Such a concept seems reasonable regardless of whether one conceptualizes the state of nature as either benign or malevolent. TLC_i is the crime rate as determined by the desire for wealth existing among individuals in the community, the crime caused by social and demographic factors, and the crime resulting from competitive or cooperative attitudes among the human species. It serves here as a theoretical construct to help understand the various components of the crime rates reported by police agencies.

Communities do not exist in isolation. Furthermore, we know criminals are capable of moving from one community to the next. Our first equation does not capture these aspects of the real world of crime. Consequently, we redefine the observed crime rate (OLC_i) as:

$$OLC_i = TLC_i - DC_i + \sum_{j \neq i} SDC_j \qquad [2]$$

where: TLC_i is the true local crime rate;

DC_i is the number of crimes deterred in the community, and $\sum_{j \neq i} SDC_j$ is the crime displaced from other communities ("spatially displaced crime").

The term $\sum_{j \neq i} SDC_j$ captures criminal movement into community i from all surrounding communities j.

The DC_i term is actually the sum of two subcomponents: potential criminal acts that are not committed due to the presence of local sanctions (globally deterred crime, or GDC_i) and criminal activity that occurs outside the community because of the presence of a relatively strong local police force (spatially displaced crime, SDC_i). The real difference between this conceptualization and that used predominantly in the deterrence literature is the term for SDC. Equation 2 may be rewritten as:

$$OLC_i = TLC_i - GDC_i - SDC_i + \sum_{j \neq i} SDC_j \qquad [3]$$

Equation 3 states that the local crime rate is equal to the true crime rate minus both those individuals leaving the life of crime and those going elsewhere to commit crimes plus the crime rate caused by those entering the community solely for illegal purposes.

This formulation requires two more qualifications. Spatially mobile crime may or may not be caused by police activity. Police-induced movement is a production externality (SDC, or spatially displaced crime). The movement of crime across jurisdictional boundaries for reasons other than police activities is termed SMC. For the sake of discussion, true local crime is separated into two subcomponents—crime committed by "new" residents ($NTLC_i$) and crimes committed by "old" residents ($OTLC_i$). Thus, we can write our final version for the observed crime rate in community i (OLC_i) as:

$$OLC_i = (NTLC_i + OTLC_i) - (GDC_i + SMC_i + SDC_i) + \quad [4]$$
$$(\sum_{j \neq i} SMC_j + \sum_{j \neq i} SDC_j)$$

where: $NTLC_i$ is the true crime rate committed by new residents;

$OTLC_i$ is the true crime rate committed by old residents;

GDC_i is the amount of globally deterred crime;

SMC_i is the crime rate of the interjurisdictional criminal who resides in but acts outside community i regardless of police practices;

SDC_i is the crime rate of the interjurisdictional criminal who resides in but acts outside community i because of police practices;

$\sum_{j \neq i} SMC_j$ is the crime rate of the interjurisdictional criminal who resides outside of but acts within community i regardless of police practices; and

$\sum_{j \neq i} SDC_j$ is the crime rate of the interjurisdictional criminal who resides outside of but acts within community i as a result of police practices.

In equation 4 we have most of the components of criminal mobility as they have been discussed in the literature. It remains to show which of these terms belong to the different perspectives on this issue. Economists and political scientists are concerned principally with the SDC component of crime rates. This emphasis is based on their concerns with production efficiency—how do we design a police service industry in the presence of fragmented political jurisdictions and spatially mobile crime?[7]

Others analyzing criminal mobility, such as urban geographers and criminologists, tend to focus on both the SMC and SDC components. That is, they are not concerned exclusively with the effect of police presence on criminal mobility, but rather in documenting its extent and striving to understand nonpolice-related reasons for such behavior.

In equation 4, crimes committed by "newly arrived" and "old" residents of community i are distinguished. This characterization of two subcomponents of the true local crime rate was added out of concern for the foci of previous empirical research efforts into questions of criminal mobility. Perhaps the phenomenon that has caused so much consternation among popular observers and suburbanites has not really been investigated. The quotation (New York *Times*, January 18, 1975: 64) with which Hakim et al. (1979) begin their article highlights the problem: "It is not a ground swell, but there is a movement of crime to the suburbs. . . . It is not surprising that urban crime rates are leveling off or dropping slightly." Hakim et al. interpret this comment, as do others, to imply a particular type of spillover of crime across jurisdictional boundaries. In particular, the literature focuses on the "quick hit and run" approach to crime, the criminal returning to his or her lair after preying on the innocent suburbanite. The rationale for such behavior is the difference in police effort of adjacent jurisdictions. Rational criminals, it is presumed, operate in locations that lessen their chances of capture, prosecution, conviction, and sentencing. Perhaps they also realize the limitations of the police power and use jurisdictional boundaries to hide behind. Yet, limited evidence supports this model of criminal behavior. Criminals minimize, if they minimize anything, travel costs. The "hit" is usually close (although not too close) to home. It seems likely that the "spillover" of crime, the movement of criminals to the suburbs, often does not include a return trip. If criminals operate in the suburbs, they probably relocated there.

This conception of crime rates is important for several reasons. First, equations 1 through 4 illustrate what assumptions must be made for observed crime rates to be used as an operational measure of police effectiveness. For example, the traditional deterrence literature assumes that crime is not displaced and that citizen reporting and police recording biases are negligible or, at most, proportionately constant. Secondly, division of the crime rate into its constituent parts permits some understanding of the different perspectives on criminal mobility that exist among those studying such behavior. Finally, it identifies two components of police productivity that have systemic consequences. These components, GDC_i and SDC_i, are positive and negative externalities, respectively. Furthermore, they are the benefits police administrators and public officials should consider in charting local police activities as well as organizing joint production or consumption groups.

CONCLUSION

This chapter provides both a brief review and a comment on the current state of the literature on criminal mobility. Prior research has provided some evidence that criminal mobility is limited, a conclusion perhaps contrary to the pronouncements of the National Advisory Commission on Criminal Justice Standards and Goals. It may be, however, that more mobile criminals are the most effective (dangerous) and most evasive. Consequently, our empirical evidence may be biased toward the more insignificant, hometown hoodlum. Some evidence suggests that the police may have some impact on whether crimes are committed locally or in adjacent localities. The question is certainly whether the magnitude of crime spillover is large even if statistically the spillover variable appears significant.

The reason that the study of criminal mobility is important is that knowledge of types of and variations in criminal activity can help local police administrators to more accurately target their resources in the battle against crime. For example, dealing with the interjurisdictional criminal might be more difficult. A number of policies to combat spillover have been suggested — the consolidation of police agencies and jurisdictions, cooperative production of police services, and complex tax and subsidy schemes. The ability of each of these mechanisms to deal with certain types of external effects is theoretically demonstrated by economists. Unfortunately, there are considerable operational and political barriers to all of these solutions. We have, at this time, little empirical basis for specific recommendations to deal with the mobile criminal.

NOTES

1. This does not imply that such changes in police manpower are efficient or cost-effective.

2. It might well be that we have a selective bias at work. Criminals who do not care about police behavior are the ones who are caught, while those who do care remain at large.

3. Emphasis on the behavior of criminals as a consequence of police activity is important. Criminals may have normal ranges of operations that are independent of and blind to the efforts of local law enforcement agencies; such spillovers are not externalities. Criminal movement across jurisdictional boundaries is a negative externality only if such movement is due to the differential production of police services in various communities. Deterrence of crime is a positive externality rather than the reduction of a negative externality because a community, in producing police services and eliminating individuals from the group of criminals, is eliminating some "natural" movement across jurisdictional boundaries that is independent of relative police effort. It is, therefore, doing its neighbors a favor that they are not paying for.

4. Our discussion of apprehension and deterrence barely dents the surface of the variety of services provided by law enforcement agencies. Ostrom et al. (1978) detail the diversity of products offered by agencies policing U.S. metropolitan areas. We have also failed to consider the multitude of positive and negative spillovers that result from the production of these services. For example, to the extent crime laboratories and detention facilities are paid for by one agency and utilized by another, positive benefits certainly accrue to the user. The sharing of

radio frequencies may have positive or negative externalities. Overloaded frequencies may impair dispatcher-squad car communication during emergencies. Alternatively, shared frequencies may yield additional information or facilitate emergency mutual aid, positive benefits to the department receiving assistance. Generally, the literature has failed to acknowledge the complexity of police service production and its consequences for community safety and security.

5. In the language of the economist, we might be studying consumption externalities in this case. Relatively wealthy neighborhoods may attract criminals from poorer areas. If they do, these neighborhoods are supplying a positive benefit to the poorer neighborhoods by reducing their crime rates.

6. A most accurate version of this definition would include a citizen reporting-police recording component. This could be included as a constant term or a proportionality constant. A complex specification might include this correction as a function of police agency characteristics and true crime rates.

7. Design of an efficient arrangement must also take the external effect of globally deterred crime into account. Actually, only a fraction of the GDC_i would potentially operate beyond the boundaries of community i. It is this fraction that is the true positive externality. However, for the sake of simplicity we will consider the entire GDC_i component a benefit to neighboring communities.

REFERENCES

AMIR, M. (1971) Patterns of Forcible Rape. Chicago: University of Chicago Press.
BLUMSTEIN, A., J. COHEN, and D. NAGIN [eds.] (1978) Deterrence and Incapacitation: Estimating the Effects of Criminal Sanctions on Crime Rates. Washington, DC: National Academy of Sciences.
BUCHANAN, J. M. and W. C. STUBBLEBINE (1962) "Externality." Economica 29 (November): 371-384.
BULLOCK, H. A. (1955) "Urban homicide in theory and fact." Journal of Criminal Law, Criminology, and Police Science 45 (January-February): 565-575.
CAPONE, D. C. and W. W. NICHOLS, Jr. (1976) "Urban structure and criminal mobility." American Behavioral Scientist 20 (November-December): 199-213.
CHAIKEN, J. M. (1976) "What's known about deterrent effects of police activities." Santa Monica, CA: Rand Corporation.
———M. W. LAWLESS, and K. A. STEVENSON (1974) The Impact of Police Activity on Crime: Robberies on the New York City Subway System. New York: Rand Institute.
CONKLIN, J. (1972) Robbery and the Criminal Justice System. Philadelphia: J. B. Lippincott.
DAHMANN, J. S. (1975) Examination of Police Patrol Effectiveness. McLean, VA: MITRE Corporation.
DEUTSCH, S. J., J. J. JAVIS, and R. G. PARKER (1979) "A network flow for evaluating and forecasting criminal displacement." Evaluation Quarterly 3 (May): 219-235.

EHRLICH, I. (1973) "Participation in illegitimate activities: a theoretical and empirical investigation." Journal of Political Economy 81 (May-June): 521-565.

FABRIKANT, R. (1979) "The distribution of criminal offenses in an urban environment: a spatial analysis of criminal spillovers and of juvenile offenders." American Journal of Economics and Sociology 38 (January): 31-47.

FORST, B. E. (1976) "Participation in illegitimate activities: further empirical findings." Policy Analysis 2 (Summer): 477-492.

GOODMAN, L. H., T. MILLER, and P. DEFORREST (1966) A Study of the Deterrent Value of Crime Prevention Measures as Perceived by Criminal Offenders. Washington, DC: Bureau of Social Research.

GREENBERG, D. F. (1977) "Crime deterrence research and social policy," pp. 281-295, in S. S. Nagel (ed.) Modeling the Criminal Justice System. Beverly Hills, CA: Sage.

_____R. C. KESSLER, and C. H. LOGAN (1979) "A panel model of crime rates and arrest rates." American Sociological Review 44 (October): 843-850.

GREENWOOD, M. J. and W. J. WADYCKI (1973) "Crime rates and public expenditures for police protection: their interaction." Review of Sociology and Economics 31 (October): 138-151.

GYLYS, J. A. (1974) "The interdependence of municipal and county police forces: an economic analysis." American Journal of Economics and Sociology 33 (January): 75-88.

HAGERTY, J. E. (1978) "Criminal justice: toward a new federal role." Public Administration Review 38 (March-April): 173-176.

HAKIM, S., A. OVADIA, E. SAGI, and J. WEINBLATT (1979) "Interjurisdictional spillover of crime and police expenditures." Land Economics 55 (May): 200-212.

Hartford Institute of Criminal and Social Justice (1979) Reducing Crime and Fear: The Hartford Neighborhood Crime Prevention Program. Washington, DC: Government Printing Office.

JONES, E. T. (1973) "Evaluating everyday policies: police activity and crime incidence." Urban Affairs Quarterly 8 (March): 267-279.

Kansas City Police Department (1978) Response Time Analysis: Executive Summary. Washington, DC: Government Printing Office.

KELLING, G. L., T. PATE, D. DIECKMAN, and C. E. BROWN (1974) The Kansas City Preventive Patrol Experiment. Washington, DC: Police Foundation.

KNAPP, F., Jr., J. A. SHARKEY, and J. R. METTS (1980) "The effects of an increase in a county sheriff's department's patrol capability." Journal of Police Science and Administration 8 (March): 5-14.

LAND, K. C. and M. FELSON (1976) "A general framework for building dynamic macro social indicator models: including an analysis of changes in crime rates and police expenditures." American Journal of Sociology 82 (November): 565-604.

LARSON, R. C. (1975) "What happened to patrol operations in Kansas City? A review of the Kansas City Preventive Patrol Experiment." Journal of Criminal Justice 3 (Winter): 267-298.

LOGAN, C. H. (1975) "Arrest rates and deterrence." Social Science Quarterly 56, 3: 376-389.

McPHETERS, L. R. and W. B. STRONGE (1974) "Law enforcement expenditures and urban crime." National Tax Journal 27 (December): 633-644.

MEHAY, S. (1977) "Interjurisdictional spillovers of urban police services." Southern Economic Journal 43 (January): 1, 352-359.

MORRIS, D. and L. TWEETEN (1971) "The cost of controlling crime: a study in economies of city life." Annals of Regional Science 5 (June): 33-49.

National Advisory Commission on Criminal Justice Standards and Goals (1973) Report on Police. Washington, DC: Government Printing Office.

NORMANDEAU, A. (1968) "Trends and patterns in the crime of robbery." Ph.D. dissertation, University of Pennsylvania.

OSTROM, E., R. B. PARKS, and G. P. WHITAKER (1978) Patterns of Metropolitan Policing. Cambridge, MA: Ballinger.

POGUE, T. F. (1975) "Effect of police expenditures on crime rates: some evidence." Public Finance Quarterly 3 (January): 14-44.

POPE, C. E. (1980) "Patterns in burglary: an empirical examination of offense and offender characteristics." Journal of Criminal Justice 8, 1: 39-51.

President's Commission on Law Enforcement and the Administration of Justice (1967) Task Force Report: The Police. Washington, DC: Government Printing Office.

PRESS, S. J. (1971) Some Effects of An Increase in Police Manpower in the 20th Precinct of New York City. Santa Monica, CA: Rand Corporation.

REPPETTO, T. A. (1976) "Crime prevention and the displacement phenomenon." Crime and Delinquency 22 (April): 166-177.

_____(1974) Residential Crime. Cambridge, MA: Ballinger.

SAMUELSON, P. A. (1955) "Diagramatic exposition of a theory of public expenditure." Review of Economics and Statistics 37 (November): 350-356.

_____(1954) "The pure theory of public expenditure." Review of Economics and Statistics 36 (November): 307-389.

SCHNELLE, J. F., R. E. KIRCHNER, Jr., M. P. McNEES, and J. M. LAWLER (1975) "Social evaluation research: the evaluation of two police patrolling strategies." Journal of Applied Behavior Analysis 8 (Winter): 353-365.

SCHNELLE, J. F., R. E. KIRCHNER, Jr., J. D. CASEY, P. H. USELTON, Jr., and M. P. McNEES (1977) "Patrol evaluation research: a multiple-baseline analysis of saturation police patroling during day and night hours." Journal of Applied Behavior Analysis 10 (Spring): 33-40.

SWIMMER, E. (1974) "Measurement of the effectiveness of urban law enforcement: a simultaneous approach." Southern Economic Journal 40 (April): 618-630.

TITTLE, C. R. and A. R. ROWE (1974) "Certainty of arrest and crime rates: a further test of the deterrence hypothesis." Social Forces 52 (June): 455-462.

TURNER, S. (1969) "Delinquency and distance," in T. Sellin and M. Wolfgang (eds.) Delinquency: Selected Studies. New York: John Wiley.

VOTEY, H. and L. PHILLIPS (1974) "The control of criminal activity: an economic analysis," pp. 1055-1093 in D. Glaser (ed.) Handbook of Criminology. Chicago: Rand McNally.

WEICHER, J. C. (1971) "The allocation of police protection by income class." Urban Studies 8 (October): 207-220.

WHITE, R. C. (1932) "The relation of felonies to environmental factors in Indianapolis." Social Forces 10, 4: 498-509.

WILSON, J. Q. (1975) Thinking About Crime. New York: Basic Books.

3

Uriel Spiegel

University of Pennsylvania
and *Bar-Ilan University*

ECONOMIC THEORETICAL VIEW
OF CRIMINAL SPILLOVER

Mehay (1977) and Hakim et al. (1979) have discussed crime displacement across jurisdictional boundaries as a result of the external effects of police expenditures. Mehay (1977) analyzes the possibility of adverse displacement of crimes across municipal boundaries, and studies the effect of police services on crime displacement while holding the level of police expenditure in other communities unchanged. Hakim et al. (1979) analyzed the displacement effect of police expenditure of every community on its crime rates as well as on those of the neighboring communities. They present a simultaneous model of supply of crime in each community, where an increase (or decrease) in police expenditure in one community causes an increase (or decrease) in police expenditure in the neighboring community, as criminal activity flows from a better-protected community to a less well-protected neighboring community. They introduce reaction curves and discuss the conditions of stable equilibrium. Their derivation of the reaction functions is based on assumed demand functions for police services as functions of crime rates. These functions are not derived from the model, but are based on intuitive argument.

This chapter extends the Hakim et al. model to establish a stable equilibrium in an interjurisdictional region with independent police departments in the presence of crime displacement. We introduce an objective function in which each community minimizes only its own social loss from criminal activity at the expense of greater criminal activity in neighboring communities. Under very basic economic conditions we derive reaction functions which lead to a stable equilibrium.

This extended model can be applied to the displacement of property crime in a given multicommunity region, and does not apply to the displacement of violent crime, for two reasons: Evaluating the cost of property crimes in monetary terms is simpler and more objective than for violent crimes, and the phenomenon of displacement is more common to property crime.

THE MODEL

We assume a region with two independent communities denoted by i and j, respectively. We use the following notation:

C_i is the property crime level in community i;
V_i is the average "social" cost of crime in community i;
P_i is the police expenditure in community i;
W_i is the wealth of community i;
E_i is the socioeconomic characteristics of community i's inhabitants; and
Π_i is the net wealth of community i.

The community maximizes its net wealth, which depends upon its private and public resources net of the social costs of crime and the resources devoted for police protection:

$$\text{Max } \Pi_i = W_i - V_i C_i - P_i \qquad [1]$$

Since W_i is given, we could view a different objective function which minimizes the last two terms of equation 1. These two terms can be regarded as the sum of the direct cost of criminal activity and the cost of police expenditure on preventing and deterring crime (T_i). This minimization problem can be expressed as:

$$\text{Min. } T_i = V_i C_i + P_i \qquad [2]$$

We assume that the average cost of crime (V_i) is a positive function of the wealth of community i (W_i). The crime rate (C_i) is a function of the levels of police expenditure in each community $(P_i$ and $P_j)$ and the socioeconomic profile of community i (E_i).

Formally, this can be written as:

$C_i = C_i(P_i; P_j; E_i)$. We assume diminishing marginal productivity of police expenditure, that is,

$$\frac{\partial C_i}{\partial P_i} < 0 \qquad \frac{\partial 2C_i}{\partial P_i 2} < 0$$

We assume, further, that the marginal productivity of the crime rate with respect to police expenditure approaches zero for levels of police protection which are smaller than the wealth of the respective community.

Police expenditure might affect criminal activity in two ways: A potential criminal will tend to reduce his criminal activity in the region and turn to legal activity because of the increased probability of being apprehended. A potential criminal may move to the neighboring community due to substitution effect, which is known as the displacement effect; that is,

$$\frac{\partial C_i}{\partial P_j} > 0 \qquad \frac{\partial C_j}{\partial P_i} > 0$$

If the challenge of Pj affects criminal activity only in community j, we should find that the gain from such internal deterrence in community j will be fully offset by an increase in criminal activity in community i.

By minimizing T_i with respect to P_i, and T_j with respect to P_j, we can introduce the following reaction functions R_i and R_j:

$$R_i: P_i = g(P_j/V_i; E_i)$$
$$R_j: P_j = h(P_i/V_j; E_j)$$

In order to analyze the equilibrium solution of the simultaneous model, we consider the properties of these functions.

The main property of the reaction functions concerns values of $g' = \dfrac{\partial P_i}{\partial P_j}$ and $h' = \dfrac{\partial P_j}{\partial P_i}$ (that is, the slopes of the reactions functions). Intuitively, it is clear that $g' > 0$ and $h' > 0$ under the assumption of crime displacement. Furthermore, we prove in the following theorem that $0 < g' < 1$ and $0 < h' < 1$ around the equilibrium. This relationship suggests that P_i decreases when P_j decreases. It is assumed, however, that it is worthwhile to the communities to have some positive police expenditure even though the neighboring communities' police expenses decline to zero.

THEOREM

There exists a level of police expenditure in community j (P_j) such that $g' < 1$; similarly, there exists a level of police expenditure in community i (P_i) such that $h' < 1$.

Proof: Using the chain rule we get:

$$g' = \frac{\partial P_i}{\partial P_j} = \frac{\partial P_i}{V_i \partial C_i} \cdot \frac{V_i \partial C_i}{V_j \partial C_j} \cdot \frac{V_j \partial C_j}{\partial P_j} \qquad [3]$$

The magnitude of g' is determined by the three terms on the right hand side of equation 3:

I. The assumption that the marginal productivity is diminishing and approaching zero for relatively small levels of police expenditure yields

$$V_j \frac{\partial C_j}{\partial P_j} > -1$$

II. $0 > \dfrac{V_i \partial C_i}{V_j \partial C_j} > -1$ by the assumption that displacement of crime is less than or equal to 100 percent.

III. The demand function for police expenditure in community i is given by: $P_i = f(C_i; V_i)$. The net benefit from police expenditure must be positive. Hence,

$$0 < \frac{\partial P_i}{V_i \partial C_i} < 1 \text{ for any level of crime.}$$

Since g' is a product of the above three factors, it must be less than one for all levels of expenditure P_j which satisfy the condition

$$0 > V_j \frac{\partial C_j}{\partial P_j} > -1.$$

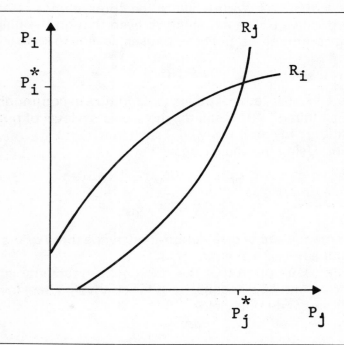

Figure 3.1   The Reaction Curves

By a similar argument $h' < 1$. It can be shown that $g' < 1$, h' < -1 and the requirement that g ($P_j = 0$) > 0 are sufficient conditions for the existence of an equilibrium (P_i^*; P_j^*). This equilibrium is depicted in Figure 3.1.

CONCLUSION

This chapter analyzes the change in a community's police expenditure in response to a change in police expenditure of a neighboring community. This interjurisdictional response has also been discussed in the work of Hakim et al. (1979), which defines the necessary conditions for equilibrium. In this chapter we have derived sufficient conditions for such an equilibrium, which are based on the objective functions of neighboring communities. The objective function each community minimizes is the social cost associated with criminal activity. That is, each community chooses independently its police expenditure, which minimizes its own social costs, including monetary losses due to local crime and monetary losses due to "imported" crime. We thereby obtained the levels of police expenditure against property crime in the case each community acts independently.

It is well known that the case in which two communities act independently is not "pareto optimal," or, in other words, they could reduce the combined cost of crime by cooperative behavior, such as by consolidating police services. This aspect of cooperation and the incentive mechanism for cooperation is an important topic for further research.

REFERENCES

BECKER, G. S. (1968) "Crime and punishment: an economic approach." Journal of Political Economy 76, 2: 169-217.
EHRLICH, I. (1973) "Participation in illegitimate activities: a theoretical and empirical investigation." Journal of Political Economy 81, 3: 521-565.
HAKIM, S., OVADIA, A., SAGI, E., and WINBLATT, J. (1979) "Interjurisdictional spillover of crime and police expenditure." Land Economics 55, 2: 200-212.
MEHAY, S. L. (1977) "Interjurisdictional spillover of urban police services." Southern Economic Journal 43: 1352-1359.

4

John A. Sorrentino, Jr.

Temple University

AN ECONOMIC THEORY OF CRIMINAL EXTERNALITIES

A change of world view can change the world viewed.

Joseph Chilton Pearce
The Crack in the Cosmic Egg

Upon entering the crime spillovers literature for the first time, one cannot help noticing the significant diversity of the models used.[1] Questions are raised that have considerable variance in generality. In this chapter we take a "systems view" to allow abstraction from specific geopolitical dimensions. The abstraction occurs to the level of the welfare economist attempting to solve a real-world problem.

A system can be thought of as a collection of animate and/or inanimate agents in interaction with each other. Each agent can be imputed to have a behavior which is subject to certain rules. A system model is an attempt to identify and specify the agents, their behaviors, their interactions, and the rules. The broadest perspective economists have used to characterize economic systems is that of general equilibrium. The most generally agreed upon welfare criterion is attributed to Pareto (1971); this criterion states that an allocation should be chosen whereby any reallocation would not make everyone at least as well off in their own estimations.

Our focus will be upon achieving a Pareto allocation in the presence of two traditional forms of market failure: public goods and externalities. The concept of public goods refers to those goods and services for which "sharing" occurs. Total consumption exceeds total production of the public good. *Pure* public goods are ones which are consumed in total by all in some relevant population. *Mixed* public goods have attributes used up by individual agents and attributes that are shared. Agents producing goods and services with any sharing face the "free rider" problem.

A universal definition of externalities is elusive. Pigou (1932) describes instances where the private costs and benefits accruing to agents are different from the concomitant social costs and benefits. He suggests systems of taxes and subsidies to "internalize" the social effects of firms' actions. In a strong critique of Pigou, Coase (1960) invokes the extreme power of the market by postulating that if negotiations are relatively costless, parties in an externality situation can achieve a Pareto solution without government interference. Baumol (1972) theoretically exonerates Pigou's tax-subsidy scheme, but claims that large numbers problems and extreme information problems preclude both Coase's and Pigou's quests for Pareto optimality. The proposal in the second section of this chapter attempts to preserve hope for Pareto optimality by reducing the informational requirements necessary to achieve it.

The collection of papers reviewed for this chapter presented many interesting welfare considerations. Mehay (1977) introduces a one-directional and nonreciprocal externality by including the police inputs of one community in the other's "production function." Hakim et al. (1979), by "proportionalizing" police expenditures into an "average-other's" decision process, create interdependent "reaction functions," but their mechanical method has little meaning in welfare economics. Gylys (1974) considers a multidistrict model with coordination at the county level. He combines the two forms of market failure into one within a two-level, systems outlook. He states that externalities occur because police services contain "indivisibilities." Since each decision depends directly on what others do, he contends that the social optimum cannot be guaranteed under separate decision making by the districts. Fabrikant (Chapter 7, this volume) adopts the perspective of Gylys in that he imagines a central law enforcement agency allocating police over communities. He assumes that *the* social cost function reduces to the strictly private dollar costs to the victims. He allows criminals to "return home with the loot." He creates a one-to-one relation between criminals and offenses by assuming that each of the former commits one of the latter per "time period" in a first-order Markov process. A social Lagrangian is used at *some* institutional level to allocate police while district-level decision making is ignored. The "weighted" social cost of the previous "time period" slips in under the guise of "expected" costs. Fabrikant deftly avoids public goods and introduces externalities by putting us into iterative time and saying that the expected *total* social costs of other disjoint districts enter the social costs of a particular district. Perhaps a different approach is more useful.

A "DIFFERENT" CRIMINAL EXTERNALITIES MODEL

Consider a four-agent system, with one designated "center" and others as "individual agents." The center has the objective of maximizing the total welfare of the group and no interest in itself. The individual units have the selfish ambition of maximizing internal welfare. Each individual performs activities and has interactions with other individuals and the center. Analogously to the laws of conservation of matter and energy, the system is closed in an "ether blanket" of total system welfare. Welfare can be dichotomized into pecuniary and nonpecuniary wealth. The former may be the "market" value of all system assets and the latter any value received beyond that reflected in the market. The task of the welfare economist is to identify the tangible and intangible assets that limit the pursuit of system well-being.

Enter market failure. The agents' decisions depend in total or at the margin on others' decisions. The lack of markets for the interactions causes supply/demand discrepancies. In our model, the center has the problem of maximizing welfare in the presence of these interactions. Some interactions are messages between the center and the agents, designed for the center to cause private decisions to conform to social objectives. The feedback loop which occurs among the agents themselves must be regulated by feedback loops of each with the center.

The Nonsharing Case. Davis and Whinston (1966) investigate a central coordination scheme to obtain Pareto optimality. It is designed to allow each agent affected by the externality interaction to propose the amount of externality it would prefer. The center would attempt to reconcile the amounts produced with the amounts desired. Appended to center objectives are constraints forcing the equality of the desired and produced levels. The shadow prices of these constraints become the basis for payments made and received by the individuals. Hence, each would choose the level of its own activity with the idea that it will either pay or receive compensation. If externalities are detrimental, then a penalty (reward) is given for over (under) supply.

Davis and Whinston preserve Pareto optimality by causing a disconnection in the interactions among the individual agents. When the center brings the desired and actual levels into equality, the artificially-disconnected interactions are restored. The shadow prices are imputed values and can serve as "externality prices."

In applying this to crime spillovers, we must be careful not to include external effects already reflected in market transactions. The use of consumer surplus in the "market" for crime control is a way to narrow the discussion to the crime spillovers literature. If net benefit from crime control is total benefit (consumers' surplus plus total expenditure) minus total cost, then consumers' surplus nets out total expenditure and total cost from benefit. Each district i has a consumer surplus relation, CS_1:

$$CS_i = f_i (K_i, A_{ij}, A_{ik}; D_{ji}, D_{ki}; M_{ci}), i, j, k = 1, 2, 3, \qquad [1]$$

where K_i is the level of internal crime-control provision, A_{ij} is the spillover from agent i to agent j, D_{ji} is the amount of spillover A_{ji} desired by i, and M_{ci} is a message from the center c to agent i. An interesting feature is that agent i is moving along its crime-control demand schedule, which itself is parametrically shifting.

Since at any point in time the spillovers themselves are disjoint, the center wants to maximize the sum of the individuals' consumer surplus. Following Davis and Whinston (1966), we can establish maximum net benefit by allowing each individual to choose the levels of spillovers imposed by others. The center has the job of imposing compliance on the producers:

$$A_{ij} = D_{ij}, i \neq j \qquad [2]$$

To judge the welfare trade-offs involved in having the A_{ij} different from the D_{ij}, the center can use the shadow prices to coordinate behavior.

The Lagrangian expression of the center's problem is

$$L = \sum_{i=1}^{3} CS_i = \sum_{\substack{i,j=1 \\ i \neq j}}^{3} Y_{ij}(D_{ij} - A_{ij}) \qquad [3]$$

The Y_{ij} are the Lagrange multiplier/shadow prices. For example, 1 gets penalized (credited) for units produced above (below) D_{12}. If 1 has to pay (get rewarded) for these units, 1 will react to these costs (payments) as well as its internal variables. Likewise, 2 will be paid for units of A_{12} above what it wants. However, 2 must pay for units of A_{12} below D_{12}. There is the need for balancing by the center. The shadow prices essentially put prices on the differences. They can be introduced into the individual agents' objectives as in equation 4.

$$CS_i = f_i(K_i, A_{ij}, A_{ik}; D_{ji}, D_{ki}) + Y_{ij}A_{ij} + Y_{ik}A_{ik} - Y_{ji}D_{ji} - Y_{ki}D_{ki},$$

$$i \neq j \neq k. \qquad [4]$$

Two of the typical first-order conditions from maximization of CS_i and CS_j exhibit the usefulness of the procedure:

$$\frac{\partial CS_i}{\partial A_{ij}} = \frac{\partial f_i}{\partial A_{ij}} + Y_{ij} = 0 \qquad [5]$$

$$\frac{\partial CS_j}{\partial D_{ij}} = \frac{\partial f_j}{\partial D_{ij}} - Y_{ij} = 0 \qquad [6]$$

Hence, $\partial f_i / \partial A_{ij} = Y_{ij} = -\partial f_j / \delta D_{ij}$. The shadow prices equate the marginal welfare loss to the spillover-recipient to the welfare gain to the spillover producer as per Pareto efficiency. The second-order conditions would hold under the correct convexity assumptions. The reader should see Lasdon (1970) for the mathematical details.

The iterative process is as follows: The center needs to monitor the A_{ij}. Mimicking a tatonnement process, iterations would occur as the center finds levels of the shadow prices that maximize the sum of consumers' surplus. Arbitrary shadow price levels start off the iterations. The individual agents send in their levels of $CS_i(1)$ and $D_{ij}(1)$, being at cross-purposes with other agents and taking into account the arbitrary shadow prices. The center sums the $CS_i(1)$ and declares that the $A_{ij}(1)$ must equal the $D_{ij}(1)$. The shadow prices generated, $Y_{ij}(1)$, are sent out to the agents. The latter adjust their $CS_i(1)$ and $D_{ij}(1)$ to $CS_i(2)$ and $D_{ij}(2)$. The iterations continue until the center gives up on a search for shadow prices that improve aggregate consumers' surplus.

Let $i = 1$; 1 has the internal problem of choosing K_1 optimally. There is some mathematical relation between K_1 and A_{12}, A_{13}, and A_{21}, A_{31}. We assume that K_1 and A_{12}, A_{13} are positively related. As the center controls A_{12} and A_{13} there will be an impact on K_1. We assume that A_{12} and A_{13} are separable in the sense that one can change without the other. Compliance with the D_{ij} will generally cause a decrease in CS_1. However, overproduction of the A_{ij} causes CS_2 and CS_3 to be lower than desired.

The Sharing Case. In the sharing case, the general CS_i function would become

$$CS_i = f_i (K_i, A_{ij}, A_{ik}, I_{ij}, I_{ik}; A_{ji}, A_{ki}, I_{ji}, I_{ki}; M_{ci}) \qquad [7]$$

The I_{ij} represent the "intersections" involved in sharing the public goods externalities. Let us get an idea of sharing by looking at agent 1 as the externality producer and agents 2 and 3 as recipients.

The sharing of the A_{12} and A_{13} is a physical or institutional phenomenon. It is physical if some physical units (such as aerial surveillance signals) are "indivisible" and used by many users at the same time. However, we can imagine public goods (such as spilled-over bullet fragments) that are appropriated by each recipient (for example, President Reagan) alone. Hence, if sharing occurs here, it must be of an institutional nature.

Assume first that the sharing is physical. The two recipients will provide D_{12} and D_{13}. Since they share some physical units, the total amount of interaction produced by 1 will be generally less than A_{12} "+" A_{13} received. Hence, the center interested in equating A_{12} with D_{12} and A_{13} with D_{13} will give 1 a socially inefficient signal. The total produced in compliance will be too low. Instead of requiring (2), the center can require:

$$A_{ij} = D_{ij} - \tfrac{1}{2}(I_{jk}), \; i \neq j \neq k \qquad [8]$$

The center must not only gather data on the A_{ij}, but the I_{jk} as well.

With sharing of an institutional nature our problems grow. The availability (*potential* use) of the good is shared. Despite the fact that the units go to single individual agents, there is an interlocking of the CS_i relations through the sharing of the availability. Availability is a pure public good.

Each agent, j, choosing D_{ij} will adjust its level according to the payments received. Even if it knew about the sharing, no agent would reduce its D_{ij} because of it. In the institutional-sharing case, we must use a price-sharing device on the shadow prices.

Whitcomb (1972) previously invoked Shoup's (1965) idea of a separate production function for externalities. We may invoke it for a separate production function for availability. If the availability is considered a joint product produced by i along with the spillover, then separate constraints can be added which would generate shadow prices on the availability. Ideally, a shadow price could be gotten which would serve to adjust the other shadow prices to take the sharing into account. A potential candidate is a simple Lindahl solution. Suppose that in a Lagrangian with some constraint involving availability we can generate shadow prices P_{jk} for I_{jk}. To cover the shared availability, recipient j would be "charged" $E \cdot P_{jk}$ while k would be "charged" $(1-E) \cdot P_{jk}$, $O < E < 1$.

An attractive aspect of the simple Lindahl solution is that the socially correct amount of the public good is produced. In the detrimental spillover case, the P_{jk} would presumably be negative to the recipients and equal to the sum of marginal benefit changes as the spillover level is changed.

APPLICATION TO CRIME SPILLOVER CONTROL

The essential question in the spillovers literature appears to be, "Ceteris paribus, at what level of consolidation do the benefits of size (economies of scale) outweigh the negative effects of spillovers?" If economics were the only consideration, then the theory of clubs, as surveyed by Sandler and Tschirhart (1980), would guide the system to the correct number of "districts" and the correct number of "citizens" in each. If we assume that there is no hope of getting all citizens in the relevant population to cooperate on any issue, then we must speak of externalities or spillovers.

The "embedding" nature of systems allows us to consider the levels at which the above spillover control mechanism can be applied. Assume that the agents 1, 2 and 3 are individual citizens. Ideally, each individual will employ private crime control to the point where additional spending equals additional expected value saved. That individuals may not, in fact, be at optimal levels is not of great importance here.

What are the spillovers at this level? Every additional "lock" employed by each party can be thought to inflict some potential crime spillover on the other two parties. These private expenditures generate virtually no economies of scale except, perhaps, in the case of an area getting a "safe neighborhood" reputation. Assuming that crime activity exists and must go somewhere, the decision of each of the parties is, "Ignoring what I do to them, are the spillover effects of the others' activities great enough for me to want to cooperate with them?" If so, then they will perhaps form a "district" or municipality at least with respect to crime control. If they do not consolidate in this fashion, something must be done to reconcile the spillovers. Their presence prevents the socially efficient use of resources.

Assume that in the spectrum from complete laissez-faire to totalitarianism, the individuals have preferences to keep crime-control activity close to the former. This is exactly the role of the Generalized Davis-Whinston Mechanism (GDWM). It allows spillovers to be reconciled with a minimum of activity from a social authority.

Although the model in the second section of this chapter can be applied at this level, we will allow our system to get more general first. Suppose that three districts form for economic and political reasons. As we have assumed less than full cooperation, each district's crime-control activity will affect the other districts. Intradistrict decisions will clash (positively or negatively) with the social good in the absence of supradistrict control. Now we are at the Gylys-Mehay-Fabrikant-Hakim et al. level of generality. Let us apply the GDWM at this level. Assume that the district-consolidation mix is fixed.

Assuming that perfect cooperation among the districts is impossible, we invoke a regional authority to oversee the crime-control activities of the districts. Gylys (1974) has the regional authority undertaking crime-control activity simultaneously (and reciprocally) with the districts. Fabrikant (Chapter 7, this volume) has the authority to make all crime-control decisions. Our model has the authority undertaking no other activity than spillovers to maximize aggregate consumer surplus.

It may be naive to assume that the regional authority has no interest in itself. At the very least, it can be expected to be interested in balancing its budget. It undertakes no crime-control activity on its own. Each district i is assumed to be able to estimate the CS_i in equation 1 from crime-control demand schedules. Each attempts to privately maximize CS_i without regard for what it does to others, but with a keen awareness of what others do to it.

Regardless of the exact specification of the spillovers, districts being hurt by others' actions and having the chance to state and be paid for their desired amounts will take advantage of it. It beats being hurt and having no control over it.

Once the desired amounts are stated, there is an effective "uncoupling" of the CS_i. This allows the authority to achieve a reasonable welfare goal by adding over the districts. The use of "reaction functions" is therefore ruled out in our model (at least for the nonsharing and physical sharing cases).

As there is no such thing as a free lunch in the presence of spillovers, we must eventually "recouple" the CS_i. The authority can do this by: (1) monitoring/estimating the spillovers that occur and (2) collecting data on the consumer surpluses and desired spillover amounts provided by spillover recipients.

There appears to be no reason for the districts to lie about the CS_i levels, as during the uncoupling they are added uniformly with others' into the welfare index. Whitcomb (1972) contains a discussion of whether "altering" the desired spillover amounts sent to the authority has an effect on efficiency in the allocation of resources. He concludes negatively. Hence, we'll assume that the information sent to the center by the spillover victims is essentially correct.

The convenient thing about the recoupling apparatus in equation 2 is that when it is imposed in equation 3 it yields shadow prices that can be used in equation 4 to coordinate behavior. As shown by equations 5 and 6, the welfare implication of every spillover is a virtual seesaw between parties. GDWM allows the seesaw to be balanced by the socially derived shadow prices.

By feeding these shadow prices back to the districts as the cost of spilling over and the gain of enduring spillovers, the authority achieves a Pareto optimal solution (at least for the nonsharing and physical sharing case) as the actual and desired levels conform.

We noted the difficulties when the spillovers are shared, as in equation 7. The physical sharing case appears to present little conceptual or mechanical difficulty with the use of equation 8. The institutional sharing is the traditional "bear" and a mechanical method of bridging equation 3 and the Lindahl pricing scheme must be found.

As noted above, the mechanical process is a computer simulation is which all iterations are done before any actual activity occurs. A time mechanism can be built in, but the complications of this will not be discussed here.

The number of crimes and the number of criminals seem to be the only two viable specifications for spillovers in our model. The relation between the two can be many-to-one, one-to-one (Fabrikant, Chapter 7, this volume), and one-to-many.

Unless they are "pinned to each other," the choice of variable has an important effect on the exact specification of the spillover. Essentially, we must create either bundles of criminals per crime or bundles of crimes per criminal. Then we must distribute one or the other among the districts.

CONCLUSIONS

The question of whether spillovers exist depends on how the problem is specified. The availability, or potential existence, of crimes and/or criminal spillovers represents institutional sharing.

If indeed, criminal spillovers are insignificant, then our model needs another home. If some or all are positive, then we apparently need only change some or all signs in the model. Good behavior needs to be *encouraged* under a Pareto scheme.

The welfare view is much more cloudy when we go from one agent's *expenditure* level to another's. Through their "proportionality manipulation," Hakim et al. (1979) get expenditures to be related but thereby submerge the crime-control technology. Fabrikant (Chapter 7, this volume) takes us back into the technology via the patrolment input, but also cannot put us into a "dense" ether blanket. Despite his uniformity of patrolmen costs across districts and private citizens, he cannot "cover" the system with linear dollars. Total system consumers' surplus is a reasonable blanket because it is semimeasurable, and, with our technique, the agents become independent. We may add consumers' surpluses over them. The center only needs to know the best estimates of the CS_i, A_{ij}, and D_{ij}.

To translate the consumer surplus welfare criterion into policy, we must be able to specify it. To net consumer surplus out of net benefit, we need a demand schedule for crime control. Assuming the law of demand holds, total value received by the agents for any level of crime control will generally exceed total expenditures.

The generality of this discussion was meant to allow the existence of a "center" at any level of government and "individuals" with various levels of complex subsystems. The choice of three agents was made to allow for spillovers and a sharing of those interactions. As the number of agents grows in the nonsharing case, the interactions are separable and additive for the center. Summing the consumer's surpluses and imposing compliance constraints become more cumbersome, especially for several iterations. The same applies for the physical sharing case with additional monitoring necessary. The "½ sharing" rule in equation 8 would need to be changed to 1/S, where S is the number of agents in the sharing set. The illusive institutional sharing case simply grows and the price sharing becomes a matter of more, and more complex, convex combinations. Of course, other potential problems increase in scale as well.

We can generalize the identities of the agents in the system from citizens to districts to countries. An example of an application of our system to countries is that of the spillovers caused by individual countries' control of global terrorism. We leave extraterrestrial systems to the imagination of the reader.

Our system has allowed us to look at cases involving criminal spillovers with the possibility of their being shared. The system was built by putting a selective review of crime spillovers literature in a welfare-economics perspective. The coordination model presented in this chapter tries to be "correct" in a welfare sense and yet provide hope for empirical research to draw the model into operational reality.

NOTE

1. The literature appeared in some need of reorganizing at a basic level. This author has written a longer version of this chapter, which presents more detail on how we built upon the shoulders of the referenced authors.

REFERENCES

BAUMOL, W. J. (1972) "On taxation and control of externalities." American Economic Review 62, 3: 207-222.

COASE, R. H. (1960) "The problem of social cost." Journal of Law and Economics 3, 1: 1-44.

DAVIS, O. A. and A. B. WHINSTON (1966) "On externalities, information and the government-assisted invisible hand." Economica 33, 131: 303-318.

GYLYS, J. A. (1974) "The interdependence of municipal and county police forces: an economic analysis." American Journal of Economics and Sociology 33, 1: 75-88.

HAKIM, S., A. OVADIA, E. SAGI, and J. WEINBLATT (1979) "Interjurisdictional spillovers of crime and police expenditures." Land Economics 55, 2: 200-212.

LASDON, L. (1970) Optimization Theory for Large Systems. New York: Macmillan.

MEHAY, S. L. (1977) "Interjurisdictional spillovers of urban police services." Southern Economic Journal 43, 3: 1352-1359.

PARETO, V. (1971) Manual of Political Economy (A. S. Schwier, trans.). New York: Augustus M. Kelley.

PIGOU , A. C. (1932) The Economics of Welfare. London: Macmillan.

SANDLER, T. and J. TSCHIRHART (1980) "The economic theory of clubs: an evaluative survey." Journal of Economic Literature 18, 4: 1481-1521.

SHOUP, C. (1965) "Public goods and joint production." Rivista Internazionale di Scienza Economiche e Commerciale 12, 3: 26-33.

WHITCOMB, D. A. (1972) Externalities and Welfare. New York: Columbia University Press.

5

Stephen L. Mehay

San Jose State University

BURGLARY SPILLOVER IN LOS ANGELES

One argument often advanced in support of consolidating local police departments in metropolitan areas is that the problem of crime displacement, caused by differentials in law enforcement levels, would be lessened by a consolidated department. Police enforcement will be one factor, among others, that will alter the reward structure perceived by potential offenders at different locations. Lower levels of police effort, for example, will tend to reduce the risk of capture and, for a given gross payoff, increase the net expected return in that jurisdiction. The variance in the distribution of police resources across jurisdictions and the lack of a regional authority to coordinate the geographical deployment of resources create the potential for crime displacement and the potential gain from a consolidated police agency.[1] The importance of such displacement and, therefore, the strength of this argument are questions that must be decided on the basis of the empirical evidence.

Previous empirical studies of crime spillovers concentrated on the effect of various risk variables on offender mobility. This approach forged a link between local police

AUTHOR'S NOTE: I would like to thank Roger Folsom, Rodolfo Gonzalez, and Geoffrey Nunn for valuable suggestions.

inputs and the arrest risk, and also permitted a direct examination of the consolidation question. The risk of arrest, however, is only one component of the expected net monetary return to crime, and it is the full "profitability" of crime that reflects actual economic incentives to potential offenders. Previous studies, by concentrating on the risk component alone, may not have estimated accurately the magnitude of urban crime spillovers.

This study attempts to fill this gap in the literature by calculating the net monetary return to burglary for a sample of districts within a given metropolitan area and employing this as an alternative measure of the actual differential in economic incentives facing potential offenders. Crime patterns are explained in terms of the relative profitability of crime undertaken at different locations. Thus, two streams of research are merged—the crime spillovers literature and the "return to burglary" literature. The next section briefly surveys previous displacement-spillover studies; the following section uses published annual data for Los Angeles police divisions to estimate the net monetary return to burglary; in the third section, a simple model of crime displacement is formulated and statistically tested using the returns to burglary measure. The final section presents a summary of the results, some tentative conclusions, and suggestions for further research.

LITERATURE REVIEW

In one of the earliest direct studies of crime displacement, Mehay (1977) analyzed the effect of differentials in police patrol levels across adjacent communities. A given "home" community, confronted with a set of contiguous communities with above-average patrol levels, would be expected to "import" property offenses. This formulation assumed that potential offenders use visible patrol as an indicator of arrest risk in various locations. An advantage of this formulation is that displacement was linked directly with police input levels. Mehay found a positive relationship between property crime rates in the "home" community and input levels in adjacent communities, but the magnitude of the displacement effect was relatively small.

While the Mehay study used data from independently policed cities, two other studies analyzed spillovers with data from areas within a single city. Mathieson and Passell (1976) examined the effect of income and arrest rates across adjacent New York City precincts. Only the income variable was statistically significant, indicating that a precinct confronted by relatively poor neighbors, as measured by median family income, could expect crime spill-ins. Furlong and Mehay (1981) constructed an index of a district's crime attractiveness using proxies for both potential crime gains (average sales per retail store and imputed rental value of houses) and risk (clearance rates). Their results indicated minor crime spillovers for the Montreal Urban Community, a consolidated department.

Hakim et al. (1979) analyzed the simultaneous interrelationship between police spending and crime. They hypothesized that adverse differentials between spending levels cause crime to be displaced, and that any crime "import" induces the recipient city to raise its own police spending. Their empirical results tend to support these hypotheses for property crime. However, this model is based on the implicit assumptions that offenders respond to police spending or that spending levels accurately reflect differences in the arrest risk. In a cross-sectional sample, expenditures may vary for many reasons unrelated to the crime deterrence activities of the police. Differences in managerial efficiency, input prices, manning and personnel policies, output mix, and unionization rates, to name a few factors, all will generate expenditure differences that will not be reflected in arrest and crime levels.

Fabrikant (1980), by using arrest data which reflected arrestees' residences as well as their crime locations, improved prior statistical estimates of the spillover phenomenon. Because these data already reflect the origin and destination of the offender, the relevant crime market within which spillovers occur—for example, contiguous areas—need not be specified in advance. The fraction of juveniles spilling from one district to another is assumed, in the model, to be determined by several independent variables which represent components of the net return to crime — transportation cost, crime payoff, and the clearance rate differential. Once again, the expected spillover effect is observed in the data, but juvenile spillovers also appear to be relatively small in magnitude.

These two results — positive but relatively minor spillover effects — are common to almost all of the previous spillover literature.[2] Thus, this literature does not provide support for the spillovers argument for consolidation. Any benefits from reduced spillovers would probably be small and possibly outweighed by the potential welfare losses imposed by consolidation schemes.

However, a second attribute shared by all of the prior research is the use of proxy variables to mirror the economic incentives prompting offenders to commit illegal acts in alternate locations. To remedy this defect and provide further evidence concerning spillovers, this study estimates the net monetary return to burglary and uses this variable to reflect the actual differential incentives confronting potential offenders and inducing mobility.

THE RETURN TO BURGLARY

In a pioneer study, Sesnowitz (1972) calculated the net monetary return to the average burglary in Pennsylvania in 1967 to be −$197. While the finding of a negative return cast some doubt on the economic model of crime, subsequent studies, including a reworking of Sesnowitz's data (Krohn, 1973a), have found positive returns to various property crimes.[3]

The approach of these studies is to calculate the expected monetary take from the average burglary in a given jurisdiction and then to subtract the monetary equivalent of the expected cost of conviction and imprisonment. Using data published by the Los Angeles Police Department (1968), we estimated the net return to burglary for districts in Los

Angeles. Following Sesnowitz, the expected net return per burglary in district i is defined as:

$$E(R)_i = G_i \cdot P(S)_i - P(I)_i \cdot C \qquad [1]$$

where G_i is the gross gain per burglary in district i, adjusted for police recovery rates, $P(I)$ is the joint probability of arrest, conviction, and imprisonment, and C is the punishment cost. The probability of success, $P(S)$, is simply $1 - P(I)$. Only the cost term, C, is constant across districts.[4]

The Gross Gain (G). The Los Angeles Police Department publishes annual data on the dollar value of reported burglary losses by each police division. This figure is adjusted for the dollar amount of property recovered by the police, and divided by the number of reported burglaries in each division to obtain the average gain per burglary in each police division. National surveys indicate that only about 50 percent of all burglaries are reported (U.S. Department of Justice, 1979).[5] Moreover, the extent of underreporting appears greater for lower-income families, which suggests a systematic variation in underreporting across city districts. However, not only the number of crimes but also the associated losses will be underreported, so that the direction of the bias for average losses will be unknown.

The Risk of Punishment P(I). The probability of arrest for burglary is calculated by dividing the number of juvenile and adult felony arrests for burglary by the number of reported burglaries. In Los Angeles County in 1970, the probability that a felony arrest would result in a felony charge was .47.[6] Once charged, the probability that a felony defendant would be bound over to Superior Court was .79, but the probability that a felony case would result in conviction was only .81. Finally, the conditional probability that a convicted defendant would receive a felony sentence was .41. It follows that the conditional probability of a felony sentence, given a felony arrest, is .12.[7] This figure can be multiplied by each district's arrest probability to arrive at the joint probability of arrest, conviction, and imprisonment.

The Cost of Punishment (C). It was found that 95 percent of all male felons in California prisons were released on parole in 1974 (California Department of Corrections, 1975). In the years 1974-1975, 290 convicts were released on parole for first-degree burglary and served an average of 45 months, while 1337 served an average of 30 months for second-degree burglary. The average time served for both types of burglary was 32 months.

To estimate foregone earnings it was necessary to obtain the personal characteristics of those sentenced to prison for burglary. In 1968, 58 percent of those sentenced were under 25 years of age, 34 percent were 25-39, and 8 percent were 40 or over. The median educational achievement was the eighth grade. Also, 56 percent of those sentenced were white, 28 percent black, and 14 percent Mexican-American. Using census data on mean earnings for persons with the above characteristics in the Los Angeles area, the annual before-tax earnings of the average sentenced burglar was estimated to be $4,804.[8] This amount is assumed lost for 32 months, the average time served, and when discounted at 1.5 percent per month, yields a present value of lost earnings of $10,106.

Due to a lack of data, several factors were omitted from the calculations which will cause both upward and downward biases in the net return figure. Upward biases are imparted because no adjustment is made for nonreporting of crime and the reporting rate is likely to be lower for crimes with small monetary losses. Second, the loss figure is not reduced to allow for the loss in value if some stolen items were fenced. Finally, the effect of multiple burglars per crime, which reduces the return per burglar, is not introduced (see Krohm, 1973a).

Of the omissions creating downward biases in the net return figure, foregone earnings are overstated because no account is taken for the effect of taxes on market earnings, nor of in-kind income received during incarceration. Also, the unemployment rate tends to be high for persons with the characteristics of convicted burglars, further reducing legal annual earnings. Finally, the arrest probability is overstated because no adjustment is made for unreported burglaries and because the effect of multiple burglars per crime is ignored. The net effect of all these omissions is unknown.

Data used to calculate the net return are presented for each district in Table 5.1; the net return appears in column 5. The average citywide return is $155. The standard deviation is $186 and indicates substantial variation across districts. It also indicates that prior studies that attempted to estimate the net return for an entire state (Sesnowitz, 1972) or country (Lees and Chiplin, 1975) will yield a misleading impression of criminal returns by glossing over the considerable interdistrict variation. Note that while the average return is positive, this is not necessary to support the economic model of offender behavior. If these calculations accurately measure the return above opportunity cost, or profit, to crime, a positive figure simply suggests positive economic profits in this industry. Indeed, if offenders were perfectly mobile and well informed about opportunities, we would expect zero economic profits in equilibrium.

A second feature of the data in Table 5.1 is that the simple correlation coefficient between the arrest probability (column 3) and the net return (column 5) is only $-.055$. This supports the original premise that using proxy variables for risk, such as the arrest rate, are unlikely to reflect actual incentives to offenders. Having obtained the calculated net return figures, it is necessary to construct a model to utilize these data in estimating interdistrict spillovers.

EMPIRICAL ANALYSIS

Let the crime supply equation in district i be specified in terms of the own-district return and the absolute differential return between i and j, where j is other districts located within the same crime "market" as i and $i \neq j$. The burglary rate in the "home" district i (B_i) is defined as:

$$B_i = f(R_i, R_j - R_i; X) \qquad [2]$$

where R_i is the net return at i, R_j is the net return in j other districts, and X is a vector of physical and socioeconomic factors.

If net returns (R_i) increase in i, B_i may rise for any one of three reasons: offenders currently in i increase their activity; former nonparticipants enter the crime market; or neighboring offenders enter i. Letting i = 1 and j = 2, these effects can be seen by evaluating:

$$\frac{\partial B_1}{\partial R_1} = \frac{\partial f}{\partial R_i} - \frac{\partial f}{\partial (R_2 - R_1)} \qquad [3]$$

Because of the first two factors, we expect $\partial f / \partial R_1 > 0$. Since increase in R_1 will reduce the differential $(R_2 - R_1)$, we would expect either an inflow of offenders or no effect at all on B_1, that is,

$$\frac{\partial f}{\partial (R_2 - R_1)} \leq 0$$

This produces the unambiguous result $\partial B_1 / \partial R_1 > 0$ even if there is little, if any, spillover effect. Changes in R_2 increase the differential and we would expect $\partial B_1 / \partial R_2 \leq 0$.

TABLE 5.1   Net Return per Burglary for Los Angeles

DISTRICTS

District	(1) Gross Return ($)	(2) Property Recovered (%)	(3) P(A)	(4) P(I)	(5) (R) Net Return ($)
Ramparts	$ 321	5.5%	.13	.0156	$140
University	231	9.1	.13	.0156	49
Hollenbeck	211	5.8	.12	.0144	51
Harbor	256	8.7	.07	.0084	147
Hollywood	648	4.0	.16	.0192	416
Wilshire	439	7.1	.10	.0120	282
West Los Angeles	1024	4.8	.27	.0324	616
Van Nuys	529	3.2	.13	.0156	346
West Valley	522	4.3	.23	.0276	207
Highland Park	265	9.3	.14	.0168	66
77th Street	227	6.6	.15	.0180	26
Newton	192	9.0	.23	.0276	−109
Venice	354	7.5	.13	.0156	164
N. Hollywood	476	4.8	.12	.0144	301
Foothill	252	6.3	.28	.0336	−112
Devonshire	350	2.8	.22	.0264	64

NOTE: P(A) is the probability of arrest and P(I) is the probability of conviction and imprisonment given arrest.

This specification admits potential spillover effects from any relevant district within the same crime market as i. For empirical analysis, however, data limitations required that a variant of this model be adopted. First, we confine the crime market to include i and those districts contiguous to i. Further, because of a small number of observations, the return to the j districts was formulated as the average for all districts contiguous to each i. Thus, equation 2 is respectified as:

$$B_i = f(R_i, D, X) \qquad [2^1]$$

where $D = \Sigma (R_j)/J - R_i$.

The effect of changes in the independent variables once again can be seen by evaluating the relevant partial derivatives. The effect of changes in R_1 on B_i is now:

$$\frac{\partial B_i}{\partial R_i} = \frac{\partial f}{\partial R_i} + \frac{\partial f}{\partial D} \cdot \frac{\partial D}{\partial R_i} \qquad [3^1]$$

The first term on the right-hand side is the effect of a change in R_i with D unchanged; we assume a compensating rise in R_j so there is no net change in D. We expect $\partial f/\partial R_i > 0$ as greater returns increase the attractiveness of criminal relative to legal activities. The second term is the effect of changes in D caused by changes in R_i. If an increase in R_i lowers D, then crime will move from j to i, assuming $\partial f/\partial D > 0$, as offenders perceive higher earnings in i. In this case, the net effect of a change in R_i on B_i is the sum of two positive effects.

However, it is possible that increases in R_i will have an alternative effect on D. For example, an increase in R_i might occur due to lax law enforcement in i. If so, offenders may perceive higher returns in *all* districts within the crime market. Thus, both R_i and R_j increase and $\partial D/\partial R_i$ will be less predictable. If the perceived increase in R is equal in all areas of the crime market, then $\partial D/\partial R_i = 0$, and there will be no net spillover effect on B_i from a change in R_i, except for the home-area effect. If the increase in R_i exceeds that in R_j, the usual spill-in to i will occur. If the increase in R_j exceeds R_i, $\partial D/\partial R_i > 0$, $\partial f/\partial D \cdot \partial D/\partial R_i < 0$ and the net effect on B_i will be unpredictable. The increase in R_i increases crime due to the home-area effect but reduces it due to a spill-out. Thus, it is possible that lax police enforcement in one district will impose costs on all districts in the crime market.

The effect of monetary returns in the home and contiguous areas is examined using data from 16 of the 17 divisions of the LAPD.[9] Burglary rate per 1000 population was estimated:

$$B_i = \alpha + \beta \, AR_i + \gamma \, R_i + \delta \, UN_i + \epsilon \, DN_i + e_i \qquad [4]$$

where AR_i is the weighted net return to burglary in j districts adjacent to i; R_i is the intradistrict return to burglary; NU_i is the unemployment rate; and DN_i the population density. AR was constructed by first inspecting maps to identify districts adjacent to each home district.[10] The average net return in the entire adjacent area was calculated by summing the net return in each individual adjacent district, weighted by the length of the shared border with the home district, and divided by the total number of individual adjacent districts for each home district. Thus, $AR_i = S \, (W_j \cdot R_j)/J$ where W_j is the exposed border length weight. The measure AR represents the average weighted net return to burglary in all areas adjacent to the home district i. It is expected that b F 0 and q J 0. The absence of time lags in the estimating equation implies that adjustments to any changes are fully completed within the given time period.

Unemployment will affect the opportunity cost of criminal activity. Since figures on unemployment rates were unavailable for individuals with similar characteristics as convicted burglars, we included UN as an explanatory variable rather than as a component of the calculated net return, R. It is expected that w J 0. Population density has been found in previous studies to affect crime rates. However, it is difficult to predict its effect a priori. Denser areas will experience more crime if more opportunities are available in a given spatial area, or less crime if detection is made easier.

The results of estimating equation 4 by ordinary least squares are presented in Table 5.2. The population density variable is omitted from the estimated equation a but included in equation b. Considering the small sample size and the use of intracity districts policed by a single agency, the equation performs well by conventional standards. The sign of the estimated coefficient for unemployment is positive with an estimated elasticity of 1.01. Burglary rates appear to be fairly responsive to current employment conditions. More important for the hypotheses advanced in this chapter, the signs of both profitability coefficients are as expected; net returns within the district have a positive effect on burglary rates while net returns in adjacent areas have a negative effect. The elasticity of the burglary rate with respect to the own-district net return, calculated at the mean, is only .04.

The coefficient of AR_i is statistically significant and suggests the presence of crime spillovers. The statistical significance of AR is improved slightly when density is omitted as an explanatory variable in a. While this result complements that of earlier studies, it is of special interest in the case of Los Angeles because the police divisions are large in both geographical area, averaging 30 square miles, and population size, averaging 180,000. A recent California survey of burglary arrestees found that 81 percent had committed their offense within five miles or less of their current residences (California Department of Justice, 1973). This suggests that the Los Angeles police districts may be so large

TABLE 5.2   Determinants of Home District Burglary Rate

	Independent Variables					
	Constant	*AR*	*R*	*UN*	*DN*	*$\bar{R}^2$*
(a) Burglaries per	−.348	−.012**	.0053	3.147**	—	
1000 population	(3.764)	(.006)	(.005)	(.414)		.82
(b) Burglaries per	1.379	−.011*	.0052	2.942**	.0003	
1000 population	(3.810)	(.006)	(.005)	(.443)	(.0002)	.83

NOTE: The numbers in parentheses are the standard errors.
 *Indicates significance at .05 level
**indicates significance at .01 level

that much of the spatial movement of offenders is obscured, except perhaps for boundary effects.[11]

As in earlier studies, the magnitude of the estimated spillover effect is relatively minor. The elasticity of the burglary rate with respect to the profitability of crime in adjacent areas, calculated at the mean, is approximately −.103, indicating a fairly inelastic response. A 10 percent decrease in adjacent returns would induce only a 1 percent increase in the home area's burglary rate, or about 35 more burglaries per year, since the average number of annual burglaries per district is 3,860. The observations were drawn from districts all policed by a single agency. Hence, we might conclude that the agency had deployed resources so as to minimize observed spillovers. That is, the volume of spillovers is less than it would have been had these districts been policed by 16 independent agencies rather than by a single agency.

Since the burglary rate was found to be responsive to differentials in monetary returns, a simple test of this hypothesis would be to examine the variance in monetary returns for two different samples, one sample composed of observations from a consolidated department, the other composed of observations drawn from nonconsolidated, independent departments. If the variance in monetary returns is significantly smaller for the consolidated sample, the implication is that consolidation would tend to reduce crime spillovers. The null hypothesis is that the variance in returns is equal for the two samples, which, if supported, would indicate that consolidation had no effect on spillovers.

To conduct this test we used the 16 divisions of the Los Angeles Police Department as the consolidated group. For the nonconsolidated group we used observations from widely dispersed, noncontiguous geographical areas under the jurisdiction of the Los Angeles County Sheriff's Department. Only if the calculated F-ratio exceeds the critical value of 2.85 can the null hypothesis be rejected, at the 5 percent significance level. The calculated F-ratio is simply the ratio of the variance in net returns for the two groups. The value of the calculated F-statistic is 1.37 and falls below the critical $F_{.05}$. Hence, we are unable to reject the null hypothesis that spillovers are similar in both consolidated and nonconsolidated environments. This analysis suggests that consolidating local police agencies will have little, if any, effect on crime spillovers.

CONCLUSION

This chapter examined the case for police consolidation based on the existence of crime spillovers in metropolitan areas where police services are provided by numerous independent, uncoordinated police agencies. Data from districts within the city of Los Angeles do not support the contention that spillovers are extensive nor that jurisdictional consolidation is likely to significantly alter the quantity of spillovers. Although an alternative measure was used to reflect economic incentives to offender mobility, the empirical results are basically in accord with those of earlier studies. Nonetheless, there are several reasons to view the results of this chapter cautiously and consider them as tentative.

First, theoretical analysis of the crime market does not indicate that spillovers will be readily observable in cross-sectional data. If this market is competitive, entry is open, and offenders are well informed, then in long-run equilibrium all supply adjustments to any earnings differentials would have been completed. Cross-sectional data would not reveal significant spillover effects from earnings differentials because these differentials would have been completed to the point where they just compensated offenders for transportion and transaction costs. Thus, a more accurate test for spillovers would be to conduct a time series analysis to determine whether spillover effects tend to change as alterations in police inputs routinely occur.

A more direct test of the effect of consolidation on spillovers will require a time series analysis. Several North American cities have carried out functional or jurisdictional consolidations in recent years and it might be possible to analyze spillovers before and after consolidation to obtain a more complete picture of its effects. There are a number of fruitful avenues of research that need to be investigated before firm policy conclusions on spatial offender behavior can emerge.

Finally, this chapter investigates only one of the numerous claims that have been made for consolidating urban police departments. A second important argument is that consolidation, especially of small departments, will lower costs due to economies of scale in police service provision.[12] If economies of scale are important in police services, then any inefficiencies due to spillovers may be minor compared to the cost disadvantages of jurisdictions that are below the optimum size. However, despite a growing body of literature,[13] the existence and strength of scale economies still remains an unresolved empirical question. Measurement of scale economies and externalities should be improved before we can make decisive recommendations concerning the deployment of local patrol forces, a move generally on consolidation of police departments. Note, too, that scale economies, even if important to police service provision, are not a sufficient reason for consolidation because small communities can always contract large-scale producers for services. Perhaps the main conclusion of this chapter is that an impressive kaleidoscope of topics awaits the efforts of future research.

NOTES

1. A second, and perhaps more important, argument for police consolidation is that of potential efficiencies due to economies of scale. Analysis of these arguments is beyond the scope of this chapter.

2. These results have been obtained from samples of "consolidated" departments—New York City, Montreal, and Los Angeles—as well as nonconsolidated environments—Southern California cities and Philadelphia suburbs.

3. Positive returns were found for grand larceny and burglary in Norfolk (Cobb, 1973), burglaries in Chicago (Krohm, 1973b), and burglaries in England (Lees and Chiplin, 1975).

4. Of course, this approach is not without problems. The formulation in equation 1 mixes the costs to *individuals* convicted of burglary with the gross return to

the average *crime* of burglary. It is impossible to estimate the gross return to the average burglar because no information is available on the actual number. As a result, the return per burglary, even if measured without error, will be a biased estimate of expected earnings per burglar. Nonetheless, for purposes of this chapter such estimates will be taken as proximate indicators of the incentives to individual offenders. At the least, direct estimates of net returns should be superior to the proxies employed in prior studies.

5. Sesnowitz (1972) arbitrarily reduces gross losses by 50 percent to account for burglars being forced to "fence" a portion of their loot and not receive the full market value. This adjustment is questionable because there is no accurate way of estimating the proportion of stolen property that is fenced. It is equally plausible that burglars will avoid stealing items that must be resold because of the additional element of risk involved.

6. All probability estimates were derived from Greenwood et al. (1973).

7. We assume that this probability is constant across districts despite evidence in Greenwood et al. (1973) which indicates some variation in sentencing practices across judges and branch courts of the county Superior Court system.

8. Although this figure may appear low, it exceeds the lowest industry earnings figure of $4496 in the Los Angeles area. It also exceeds the figure used by Sesnowitz (1972) for a comparable time period.

9. Central Division was excluded because land use is predominantly commercial and not comparable to the other divisions.

10. Comparable data on burglary losses of adjacent areas policed by the L.A. County Sheriff's Department were available and thus used in this study (Los Angeles County Sheriff's Department, 1969). Areas policed by independent cities were omitted due to a lack of comparable data.

11. Note that we can only infer that the higher burglary rates in districts surrounded by adjacent areas with lower returns are caused by spill-ins from the lower return areas. However, it appears reasonable to conclude that some portion of the higher crime can be attributed to displaced offenders.

12. Other arguments are that consolidation will raise professional standards, reduce duplication, and increase service uniformity and quality. (See, for example, Advisory Commission on Intergovernmental Relations, 1974; Committee for Economic Development, 1972; President's Commission on Law Enforcement and Administration of Justice, 1967.)

13. For a recent survey of the empirical evidence on scale economies in police services see Fox (1980).

REFERENCES

Advisory Commission on Intergovernmental Relations (1974) American Federalism: Into the Third Century. Its Agenda. Washington, DC: Government Printing Office.

_____ (1963) Performance of Urban Functions: Local and Areawide. Washington, DC: Government Printing Office.

California Department of Corrections (1975) California Prisoners, 1974, 1975. Sacramento: Author.

California Department of Justice, Bureau of Criminal Statistics (1973) The Burglar in California: A Profile. Research Report No. 15. Sacramento: Author.

COBB, W. (1973) "Theft and the two hypotheses," pp. 19-30 in S. Rottenberg (ed.) The Economics of Crime and Punishment. Washington, DC: American Enterprise Institute.

Committee for Economic Development (1972) Reducing Crime and Assuring Justice. New York: Author.

FABRIKANT, R. (1980) "Interjurisdictional spillovers of urban police services: comment." Southern Economic Journal 46 (January): 955-961.

FOX, W. (1980) Size Economies of Local Government Services: A Review. Rural Development Research Report No. 22. Washington, DC: USDA.

FURLONG, W., and S. MEHAY (1981) "Urban law enforcement in Canada: an empirical analysis." Canadian Journal of Economics 14 (February): 44-57.

GREENWOOD, P.W., S. WILDHORN, E.C. POGGIO, M.J. STRUNWASSER, and P. DeLEON (1973) Prosecution of Adult Felony Defendants in Los Angeles County: A Policy Perspective. Santa Monica, CA: Rand Corporation.

HAKIM, S., A. OVADIA, E. SAGI, and J. WEINBLATT (1979) "Interjurisdictional spillover of crime and police expenditure." Land Economics 55 (May): 200-213.

KROHM, G. (1973a) "An alternative view of the returns to burglary." Western Economic Journal 11 (September): 364-367.

_____ (1973b) "The pecuniary incentives of property crime," pp. 31-34 in S. Rottenberg (ed.) The Economics of Crime and Punishment. Washington, DC: American Enterprise Institute.

LEES, D. and B. CHIPLIN (1975) "Does crime pay?' Lloyds Bank Review (April): 30-39.

Los Angeles County Sheriff's Department (1969) Statistical Summary 1968-69.

Los Angeles Police Department (1968) Management Services Division. Statistical Digest.

MATHIESON, D. and P. PASSELL (1976) "Homicide and robbery in New York City: an economic model." Journal of Legal Studies 5 (January): 83-98.

MEHAY, S. (1977) "Interjurisdictional spillovers of urban police services." Southern Economic Journal 43 (January): 1352-1359.

President's Commission on Law Enforcement and the Administration of Justice (1967) The Challenge of Crime in a Free Society. Washington, DC: Government Printing Office.

SESNOWITZ, M. (1972) "The return to burglary." Western Economic Journal 10 (December): 477-481.

U.S. Department of Commerce (1970) Bureau of Census, Characteristics of the Population 1970, Part 6, California: Section 2. Washington, DC: Government Printing Office.

U.S. Department of Justice (1979) Sourcebook of Criminal Justice Statistics, 1978. Washington, DC: Government Printing Office.

6

Lee R. McPheters
Arizona State University
William B. Stronge
Florida Atlantic University

CRIME SPILLOVER IN THE BOSTON AREA

Control of criminal activity has been a major objective of citizens and legislators for decades. Public expenditures on crime control, as reported by the U.S. Department of Justice (1980), exceeded $25 billion in 1979, providing an inflation-adjusted increase in such expenditures of 67 percent since 1971. Meanwhile, both crime levels and crime rates continued to rise over this period, with more than 12 million crimes reported in 1979 (Federal Bureau of Investigation, 1980).

One aspect of the crime problem that seems to inhibit overall crime reduction is fragmentation of crime control efforts at all levels. For example, legislators may enact stricter criminal codes with stiffer penalties for crime in the belief that such penalties will deter potential offenders. But, because strong incentives exist for both prosecutors and offenders to negotiate plea agreements, these arrangements may very often result in reduced sentences which weaken the deterrent impact of the crime control legislation (Heumann, 1978). And, once sentences are meted out, correctional authorities and parole boards are free to alter them. It is rare that criminals actually serve the full sentence as prescribed by the court.

Recognizing that the courts and correctional system may not be providing levels of punishment sufficient to deter a large volume of crime, potential victims act to harden crime targets. An individual homeowner may improve his or her locks and exterior lighting, hoping to reduce the probability of becoming a burglary victim. However, it is likely that this effort will simply displace crime to his neighbor, rather than reduce the general level of criminal activity.

Similarly, the economist's view of the criminal as a rational maximizer weighing costs and benefits of various legal and illegal alternatives suggests that efforts by a single police jurisdiction to upgrade its levels of crime deterrent efforts may cause displacement of crime to neighboring communities. Potential offenders will devote less time to crime opportunities in higher risk areas and instead will prefer to move into relatively lower risk areas. This issue has received substantial attention from policy makers and analysts concerned with crime control. If displacement does occur, this may be offered as an argument in support of consolidation of police departments, which now provide independent and fragmented services in many metropolitan areas (President's Commission on Law Enforcement and Administration of Justice, 1967).

This chapter is an empirical study of the significance of such interjurisdictional spillovers in the Boston metropolitan area. The approach used is similar to that of Mehay (1977), but also draws upon a model of urban criminal activity which we used in the past (McPheters and Stronge, 1974). In the following section, this model is presented and the data from the Boston area are discussed; the estimation results follow. In the fourth section, these results are evaluated in light of a formal discussion of some of the econometric assumptions behind the emerging spillover literature. A brief reformulation of the model in a set of simultaneous equations is next presented and the conclusions to the study round out the chapter.

EMPIRICAL ANALYSIS

While interjurisdictional spillovers of positive and negative externalities and the effects these might have on resource allocation within the public sector have been of interest to a number of analysts (Barlow, 1970; Brainard and Dolbear, 1967; Hirsch, 1964; Hirsch and Marcus, 1969; Isserman, 1976), detailed treatment of spillovers in law enforcement was absent until the path-breaking work of Mehay (1977). Examining 46 cities in the Los Angeles area, Mehay found that variations in crime in individual communities were empirically related to variations in police inputs in neighboring communities. Mehay (1977: 1355) expressed the police input variable, d_i, as a differential between any given community and the average of its neighbors:

$$d_i = \sum_{j=i}^{N} (l_j/P_j)/n - (l_i/P_i)$$

where the police input variable, I, was measured as the number of sworn officers on street patrol, and P measured population.

Although there have been recent reformulations and extensions of Mehay's original approach (Fabrikant, 1979; Hakim et al., 1979), there have been to date no specific attempts to analyze the validity of a central postulate of the Mehay model, the differential law enforcement input variable. The explanatory power of the law enforcement input variable seems questionable. Appearing as an independent variable in an equation explaining crime rates in community i, the differential input variable, d_i, implies that an additional patrol officer per capita in the average of neighboring communities has the same effect on local crime rates as an additional patrol officer per capita in the local community (but with opposite sign in the presence of positive crime displacement). We believe the Mehay formulation of the law enforcement input variable as a differential composite variable introduces a restriction which lacks theoretical justification and may actually obscure the true nature of the displacement process.

To see the essence of the theoretical problem, consider a metropolitan region of many jurisdictions. Assume that crime in the region is reduced as the total level of metropolitan law enforcement activity increases. Within each jurisdiction, increases in local law enforcement activity are assumed to deter (and also displace) local crime. In order for the regional crime level to decline as regional law enforcement activity increases, it must follow that the positive spillover effects of displaced crime among the respective jurisdictions are smaller in absolute value than the absolute value of the negative effects of local enforcement activity on local crime. Aggregating over all jurisdictions, the negative deterrent effects of increases in local enforcement activity on local crime will exceed (rather than equal) the positive spillover effects of neighboring activity on local crime. (For proof of this proposition in a two-jurisdiction model, see Hakim et al., 1979: 202.) Because of this theoretical inconsistency, we expressed the spillover process in both restricted (composite variable) and unrestricted (independent law enforcement activity variables) form in our empirical tests.

Our starting point for the analysis was a deterrence function in which crime in community, C_i, per unit of population, Q_i, is expressed as:

$$C_i Q_i = f(E_i C_i, P_{1i}, P_{2i}, \ldots, P_{ni}) \qquad [1]$$

where E_i indicates law enforcement effort in community i, and $P_{1i}, \ldots P_{ni}$ are exogenous socioeconomic determinants of crime in that community.

As pointed out by Mehay (1977: 1358), measures of law enforcement activity may be formulated in a number of ways, including arrest, clearance, conviction rates, or in terms of law enforcement expenditures. We believe the last variable, adjusted by the volume of reported crime, most accurately quantifies overall law enforcement activity levels in a jurisdiction.

Equation 1 can be regarded as a partial reduced form in which all of the right-hand side endogenous variables except E_i/C_i have been solved out and, therefore, replaced by these exogenous determinants. All exogenous variables are expressed as rates or per capita to adjust for differences in size and prevent heteroscedasticity in the disturbances.

Following the Mehay formulation of the displacement process in law enforcement activity, we expressed the displacement to be estimated for the ith community as

$$C_i/Q_i = f\,(E_i/C_i - \sum_{j=1}^{n} (E_j/C_j)/n,\, P_{1i},\, P_{2i},\, \ldots,\, P_{ni})$$

$$= f\,(ED_i,\, P_{1i},\, P_{2i},\, \ldots,\, P_{ni}) \qquad [2]$$

where ED_i is adopted as a convenient notation for the differential in law enforcement activity between community i and the average of its neighbors. Given positive crime displacement effects, decreases in ED for community i should lead to increases in the crime rate in i.

The socioeconomic data consisted of 18 variables from the 1970 census for 91 towns in the Boston area. These towns were all within 30 miles of the central city. All had populations of at least 10,000 persons. Data on 18 variables measuring public expenditures and municipal revenue and debt were obtained from the 1972 Census of Governments.

The spatial coordinates of the centers of the towns were obtained from the Commercial Atlas and a matrix of intertown straight line distances was calculated. The matrix was used to identify each town's neighbors. Our software permitted us to choose neighbors on the basis of any arbitrary distance, and after some experimentation we selected a distance of 6.5 miles between town centers to provide our definition of neighboring towns. The results seemed to be broadly insensitive to variations in the distance criterion.

Total index crimes in 1972 and burglaries were selected as the crime variables for the analysis. The use of total index crimes was consistent with the use of total police expenditures as the effort variable. Burglaries were also included since there is previous evidence that this crime type is particularly influenced by spillover effects (Hakim et al., 1979: 210).

To avoid potential problems of multicollinearity, the matrix of socioeconomic variables was collapsed into a smaller subset of orthogonal vectors using a principal components procedure. These components were then introduced as separate independent variables in the regression analysis. Components with eigenvalues of a least unity were included, and the resulting four components accounted for 83 percent of the total variation in the original socioeconomic data matrix. Loadings on each component are shown in Table 6.1.

The first principal component can be interpreted as an index of poverty or economic deprivation in a community. The second principal component can be interpreted as an index of age of the community's inhabitants. Immigration from foreign countries to this area has slowed in recent years, so that the elderly cohorts contain a higher proportion of people who are foreign born. The third component

TABLE 6.1   Principal Components of Boston Area Socioeconomic
             Data, 1970

Loadings on First Principal Component (POVERTY)	
Median family income	−.94
Percentage families below poverty	.84
Median education	−.91
Percentage unemployed	.80
Percentage white-collar employment	−.85
Percentage families with income $15,000+	−.95
Percentage housing owner-occupied	−.78
Median rooms/owner-occupied	−.85
Median value housing	−.81
Median contract rent	−.82
Loadings on Second Principal Component (AGE)	
Median age	.69
Families with children	−.64
Percentage foreign born	.68
Loadings on Third Principal Component (WHITE)	
Percentage families	.90
Percentage nonwhite	−.75
Loadings on Fourth Principal Component (GROWTH)	
Percentage change population 1960−1970	.95

can be interpreted as an inverse measure of nonwhite, that is, a measure of the relative importance of the white population in a community. The fourth component contains only one significant loading, on the population growth variable.

ESTIMATED RESULTS

The results of estimating equation 2 are shown in the first two rows of Table 6.2. The hypothesized signs of each variable are shown in the row across the top of the table. Standard errors are written below the coefficients.

The displacement variables enter the two crime equations with the hypothesized sign, supporting the displacement hypothesis for the Boston area. Of the socioeconomic components, only WHITE is significant in both equations. The POVERTY variable is also significant in the explanation of total crime. The effort differential variable was significant in both equations, suggesting that a rise in local, relative to neighborhood, effort would deter crime.

Pitfalls in the Differential Variable Displacement Formulation

Although the results reported in the first two rows of Table 6.2 seem to suggest the existence of crime displacement, the specification of the displacement effect through the use of a differential variable may obscure the true results. In fact, it can be shown that the regression coefficient on the differential variable may be an estimate of the true regression on local effort alone, and its standard error may also be an estimate of the simple regression's standard error.

Consider the situation where we estimate

$$Y = \beta_0 + \beta(X_1 - X_2) + U \qquad [3]$$

and the true model is

$$Y = \beta_0 + \beta_1 X_1 + \beta_2 X_2 + U = \beta_0 + \beta_1 X_1 + U \qquad [4]$$

TABLE 6.2 Regression Results: Crime and Law Enforcement Expenditures

	Constant	POVERTY	AGE	WHITE	GROWTH	E_i/C_i	$(E_i/C_i)n$	ED	R^2
		(+)	(+)	(−)	(+)	(−)	(+)	(−)	
(1) Burglary	.011 (.0004)	.022 (.001)	.001 (.002)	−.005 (.002)	.002 (.003)			−.00001 (.000002)	.49
(2) Total	.030 (.001)	.006 (.002)	.012 (.014)	−.021 (.005)	.011 (.007)			−.017 (.002)	.70
(3) Burglary	.012 (.001)	.002 (.001)	.001 (.002)	−.006 (.002)	.003 (.003)	−.00001 (.000002)			.50
(4) Burglary	.013	.002	.001	−.006	.003	−.00001	−.00001		.50
(5) Total	.047 (.002)	.006 (.002)	.018 (.004)	−.022 (.005)	.014 (.007)	0.017 (.002)			.73
(6) Total	.047 (.002)	.006 (.002)	.018 (.004)	−.022 (.005)	.013 (.007)	−.017 (.002)	.0009 (.007)		.73
(7)[a] Burglary	.015	.001	.002	−.005	.002	−.00002	−.00002		.41
(8)[a] Burglary	.012 (.008)	.002 (.001)	.002 (.002)	−.004 (.003)	.001 (.003)			−.00002 (.000008)	.40
(9)[a] Total	.051 (.022)	.010 (.010)	.015 (.008)	−.029 (.018)	.020 (.018)	−.006 (.027)	−.017 (.051)		.52
(10)[a] Total	.032 (.003)	.004 (.006)	.015 (.007)	−.017 (.009)	.008 (.010)			−.024 (.014)	.63

NOTE: Figures in parentheses are standard errors.
a. Estimated by two-stage least squares.

where $\beta_2 = 0$.
The least squares estimator for β is

$$\hat{\beta} = W_1\hat{\beta}Y_1 - W_2\hat{\beta}Y_2 \qquad [5]$$

where we define

$$W_i = S^2{}_{xi}/S^2{}_{x1-x2}$$
$$\hat{\beta}_{Yi} = S^2{}_{Yxi}/S^2{}_{xi} \quad i = 1, 2$$

and S^2 is used to denote a variance or covariance. The normal equations for a multiple regression tell us that

$$(1 - R^2)\hat{\beta}_1 = \hat{\beta}_{Y1} - \hat{\beta}_{21}\hat{\beta}_{Y2} \qquad [6]$$

where R^2 is the squared multiple correlation of X_1 and X_2, and $\hat{\beta}_{21}$ is the ordinary least squares estimator of the regression of X_2 on X_1. Substituting equation 6 into equation 5 yields

$$\hat{\beta} = a_1\hat{\beta}_{Y1} + a_2\hat{\beta}_1 \qquad [7]$$

where

$$a_1 = W_1 - W_2/\hat{\beta}_{21} = W_1 - W_1/\hat{\beta}_{12} = (\hat{\beta}_{12} - 1)W_1/\hat{\beta}_{12}$$
$$a_2 = W_2(1 - R^2)/\hat{\beta}_{21} - (1 - R^2)W_1/\hat{\beta}_{12}$$

$\hat{\beta}_{12}$ is the regression of X_1 on X_2. From equation 7 the expected value of $\hat{\beta}$ is

$$E\hat{\beta} = a_1E(\hat{\beta}_{Y1}) + a_2E(\hat{\beta}_1) = (a_1 + a_2)\hat{\beta} \qquad [8]$$

using equation 4 to calculate $E(\hat{\beta}_{Y1})$ and noting that "overspecification" does not bias a regression estimator (Wonnacott and Wonnacott, 1970: 415-417). The bias of $\hat{\beta}$ is

$$E(\hat{\beta}) - \beta_1 = (a_1 + a_2 - 1)\beta_1$$

but $a_1 + a_2$ is a positive fraction so that the estimator $\hat{\beta}$ is downward biased:

$$a_1 + a_2 = (\hat{\beta}_{12} - R^2)\, W_1 / \hat{\beta}_{12} = (S^2_{x1} - S^2_{x1x2}) / S^2_{x1-x2}$$

and $S^2_{x2} - S^2_{x1x2} > 0$. The bias will be larger, the larger is S^2_{x2} relative to S^2_{x1x2}. If S^2_{x2} is close to S^2_{x1x2}, the bias will be very small.

The variance of $\hat{\beta}$ is (from equation 7)

$$V(\hat{\beta}) = a^2_1 V(\hat{\beta}_{Y1}) + a^2_2\, V(\hat{\beta}_1) + 2a_1 a_2 COV(\hat{\beta}_{Y1}, \hat{\beta}_1)$$

but given fixed X_1 and X_2 $\hat{\beta}_1$ and $\hat{\beta}_{Y1}$ will be uncorrelated in repeated samples. Also

$$V(\hat{\beta}_1) = V(\hat{\beta}_{Y1}) / (1 - R^2)$$

An overspecified model inflates the variances. Hence

$$V(\hat{\beta}) = [a_1 = 2a_1 a_2 + a_2 / (1 - R^2)]V(\hat{\beta}_{Y1}) = [(a_1 + a_2)^2$$

$$+ R^2 a^2 / (1 - R^2)]V(\hat{\beta}_{Y1})$$

Thus, using $V(\hat{\beta})$ to estimate $V(\hat{\beta}_{Y1})$ may lead to a bias in either direction, since the term in square brackets can be greater or less than unity.

These results indicate that it is possible to obtain accurate estimates of β_1 and $V(\beta_1)$ from a regression of the form (3). That is, if the true relationship does not involve X_2, a regression using the differential $X_1 - X_2$ as the independent variable can provide a significant coefficient, but this coefficient is a (biased) estimate of the simple regression coefficient on X_1 alone.

Rows 4 and 6 of Table 6.2 show that when the local and neighboring police effort variables are entered separately in the regressions for the two crime variables, the neighboring variable is insignificant. In the case of burglary it has the wrong sign. Note also that the adjusted coefficient of determination increases.

In order to check for possible multicollinearity problems, we estimated the equations including local effort alone (rows 3 and 5) and the results were identical to the cases in which the neighborhood valuables were included. Thus, the lack of significance of the neighborhood variables did not result from an intercorrelation with the local variables.

These results suggest that the support for the displacement hypothesis is in fact spurious. It is due to the specifications of the variables as differentials, and vanishes when the variables are entered separately.

Since the data sets and variables used here differ from those of Mehay (1977), we are unable to comment directly on the validity of the crime displacement findings of his previous study. However, the present results strongly suggest the existence and strength of displacement effects may be sensitive to the formulation of the measure as a differential variable.

SIMULTANEOUS EQUATION BIAS

The preceding results follow Mehay (1977) by assuming no simultaneous bias in the estimation of equation 2 in differential or separated variables form. It may be argued that the relationship is simultaneous because communities react to an increase in the crime rate by expanding police effort. Mehay considered this possibility, but argued that the reaction occurred with a lag so that simultaneity bias was not present. However, this implies irrational expectations on the part of community policy makers, because they are assumed to adapt to criminal displacement, rather than forecast them on the basis of the budgets adopted in neighboring communities.

The deterrence function (2) with the variables entered separately can be regarded as part of a simultaneous system as follows:

$$\left(\frac{C_1}{Q_i} = f\left(\frac{E_i}{C_i}, \frac{NE_i}{NC_i}, P_{1i}, \ldots, P_{ni} \right) \right) \qquad [9]$$

$$\frac{E_i}{C_i} = g\left(\frac{C_i}{Q_i}, B_i, \frac{NE_i}{NC_i}\right) \qquad [10]$$

$$B_i = h\left(P_{1i}, \ldots, P_{ni}\right) \qquad [11]$$

$$\frac{NC_i}{NQ_i} = F\left(\frac{NE_i}{NC_i}, \frac{E_i}{C_i}, NP_{1i}, \ldots, NP_{mi}\right) \qquad [12]$$

$$\frac{NE_i}{NC_i} = G\left(\frac{NC_i}{NQ_i}, NB_i, B_i\right) \qquad [13]$$

$$NB_i = H\left(NP_{1i}, \ldots, NP_{mi}\right) \qquad [14]$$

where neighborhood variables begin with N and neighborhood functional relationships are denoted by upper-case letters.

Equation 10 is a local reaction function assuming that the community expands police effort as its crime rate rises or as the neighborhood police effort increases. The variable B_i is the local community public budget, and acts as a constraint on police expenditure. This variable is dependent on the socioeconomic characteristics of the community as noted in equation 11. Equations 13-15 are the neighborhood equations corresponding to equations 10-12.

In order to estimate equation 9 by two-stage least squares we need the reduced form equations for local and neighborhood police effort. These "first stage" equations are obtained by regressing the two variables on all the exogenous variables of the system, that is, on $P_1 \ldots P_n$, NP_1, $\ldots$, NP_m.

We summed the census variables in each neighborhood and applied a principal components analysis as before. We obtained two components, with the first accounting for 86 percent of the variation. Our results are sensitive to the summing of rates and percentages — and, with more resources, we would have preferred to operate on the raw data as we did in computing neighborhood crime and police expenditure variables. The results of applying 2SLS with the six principal components as exogenous variables are given in rows 7-10 of Table 6.2.

The results for burglary (rows 7 and 8) are virtually the same as in the ordinary least squares estimations. When the effort variables are entered as a differential the sign on the displacement variable is correct and significant. When the variables are entered separately, the neighborhood variable is insignificant and has the "wrong" sign.

In the case of total crimes, the differential variable has the right sign but is no longer significant. When the variables are entered separately, the neighborhood variable has the wrong sign and is insignificant. The local effort variable is also insignificant although it has the right sign.

CONCLUSION

Although the Boston area data appeared to support the hypothesis of crime displacement resulting from neighboring law enforcement activity, further analysis suggested that the results were spurious. Expressing the law enforcement effort measure as a composite differential variable imposes a restriction which is not theoretically grounded and results in an estimated coefficient for this variable which is a biased estimate of the simple regression coefficient on local enforcement activity alone. When neighboring enforcement effort was entered separately it was insignificant and usually had the wrong sign. Correction for multicollinearity and simultaneity bias did not alter these conclusions.

The evidence presented here for the Boston area indicates that the influence of neighboring enforcement activity on local crime may be negligible. At best, displacement effects appear too small to be measured with our data and methodology. These results are not necessarily totally inconsistent with other studies reporting the existence of displacement of crime and law enforcement, since these effects usually tend to be very small. Alternative definitions of neighboring communities or a different formulation of the spillover process may have yielded more positive results for the Boston area. At present, however, we are left with a very traditional policy conclusion: The major deterrent to local criminal activity is local deterrent effort by enforcement agencies, and the benefits of police consolidation in terms of displacement reduction appear minimal.

REFERENCES

BARLOW, R. (1970) "Efficiency aspects of local school finance." Journal of Political Economy 78, 5: 1028-1040.

BRAINARD, W. C. and F. T. DOLBEAR (1967) "The feasibility of oversupply of local public goods: a critical note." Journal of Political Economy 75, 1: 86-90.

FABRIKANT, R. (1979) "The distribution of criminal offenses in an urban environment: a spatial analysis of criminal spillovers and of juvenile offenders." American Journal of Economics and Sociology 38, 1: 31-47.

Federal Bureau of Investigation (1980) Uniform Crime Reports: Crime in the United States, 1979. Washington, DC: Government Printing Office.

HAKIM, S., A. OVADIA, E. SAGI, and J. WEINBLATT (1979) "Interjurisdictional spillover of crime and police expenditure." Land Economics 55, 2: 200-212.

HEUMANN, M (1978) Plea Bargaining. Chicago: University of Chicago Press.

HIRSCH, W. A. (1964) "Local vs. area-wide urban government services." National Tax Journal 17 (December): 331-339.

_____ and M. MARCUS (1969) "Intercommunity spillovers and the provision of public education." Kyklos 22, 4: 641-680.

ISSERMAN, A. (1976) "Interjurisdictional spillovers, political fragmentation and the level of local public services: a re-examination." Urban Studies 13 (February): 1-12.

McPHETERS, L. and W. STRONGE (1974) "Law enforcement expenditures and urban crime." National Tax Journal 27 (December): 633-644.

MEHAY, S. (1977) "Interjurisdictional spillovers of urban police services." Southern Economic Journal 43 (January): 1352-1359.

President's Commission on Law Enforcement and the Administration of Justice (1967) The Challenge of Crime in a Free Society. Washington, DC: Government Printing Office.

U.S. Department of Justice (1980) Justice Expenditure and Employment in the U.S., 1979. Washington, DC: Government Printing Office.

WONNACOTT, R. and T. WONNACOTT (1970) Econometrics. New York: John Wiley.

7

Richard S. Fabrikant
University of Denver

POLICE ALLOCATION IN THE
PRESENCE OF CRIME SPILLOVER

The response of criminals residing in contiguous communities to an alteration in the allocation of law enforcement resources can take the following forms: the reduction or increase in the number of crimes each criminal commits; the deterrence or enhancement of future criminal entrants; or the redistribution of criminal activity among communities. This redistribution or displacement phenomenon creates positive or negative externalities resulting in a decrease or increase in the offense rate in the individual community (Press, 1971; Mehay, 1977; Fabrikant, 1979; Hakim, 1980). If the existence of these externalities is not taken into account by the law enforcement agency in determining an optimal allocation of police manpower, then the outcome will be nonoptimal (Fabrikant, 1977).

The traditional specification and statistical estimation of a solution for the law enforcement resource allocation problem is significantly constrained by the availability of comparable time series observations. This difficulty becomes even more severe when the model is formulated in a dynamic intertemporal framework.

The purpose of this study is to analyze, utilizing a systems simulation approach based on Howard (1960), a dynamic optimization program which economized on data and results in an optimal solution to the allocation problem. The first part of this presentation describes the three basic steps included in the optimization procedure. The first step, termed Cost Determination, is an evaluation of expected costs of offenses, given various behavioral assumptions regarding criminal movement among communities. The second step, Policy Determination, takes into account the responses of criminals to the new police allocation. Once this step is completed, a new expected cost of offenses is ascertained and compared to the previous one. If it is less, an improvement has been made and a new optimal allocation of police is attempted. If it is not, the previous allocation is maintained. A schematic representation of this procedure is shown in Figure 7.1.

The empirical estimation of the response functions included in the optimization procedure is then presented. The problems associated with the crime data and the empirical testing of the response functions are described. This is followed by the specification of the functional forms and the results of estimating these equations using data from the city of Los Angeles. Finally, a simulation of the actual opti-

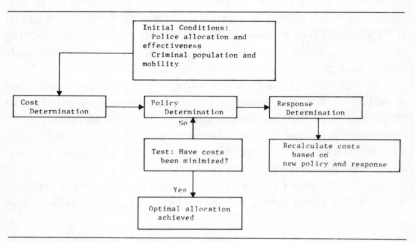

Figure 7.1   The Optimization Process

mization procedure is carried out. The results of this simulation are shown to support the hypothesis that unless crime displacement is taken into account, a nonoptimal allocation of police patrols is obtained.

THE STRUCTURE OF THE OPTIMIZATION PROCEDURE

In the present analysis, the cost of criminal activity is assumed to be the cost per illegal activity which can be directly assigned to the criminal as reported and used for police patrol allocation purposes by the police department.[1] For example, if criminals residing in Community X commit offenses only in Community Y, the cost apportioned to criminals in X will be derived from their activity in Y.

The movement of criminals among communities is assumed to be described by a Markov process. This implies that the probability of a criminal committing his or her next crime in any given community is dependent upon his or her present location but independent of any past offense history. Furthermore, it is assumed that a criminal commits one crime per discrete time period where each time period is of equal duration. This is represented by the conditional probability a_{ij}, the probability that a criminal presently in community i will commit his or her next offense in community j, where:

$$\sum_{j=1}^{k} a_{ij} = 1 \text{ and } 0 \leq a_{ij} \leq 1, \text{ where } i = 1, \ldots, k \qquad [1]$$

The transition matrix of conditional probabilities is termed the Criminal Mobility Matrix.

Each transition by a criminal represents the commission of a crime and thus, a cost to society. Hence the cost structure becomes a random variable with a probability distribution governed by the relations of the Criminal Mobility Matrix. By multiplying the Criminal Mobility Matrix with the cost per crime in each community, C_j, the assignment of costs to the criminals residing in each community is derived. In this manner, the cost of illegal activity is centered at the source or cause of that activity, rather than on the location of the outcome.

Once the criminal mobility matrix, cost matrix, and expected costs are specified, the problem becomes one of deriving the total cost to society if the criminal activity persists over the next "n" time periods. This is done by solving the set of equations:

$$TC_i(n) = q_i + \sum_{j=1}^{k} a_{ij}TC_j(n-1) \qquad [2]$$

where: n = the number of time periods,
$i = 1, \ldots, k$, and
$$q_i = \sum_{j=1}^{k} a_{ij} C_j.$$

$TC_i(n)$ is the total cost in time period n generated by a criminal starting in community i, C_j is the cost per criminal transition, and a_{ij} the conditional transition probability. Thus, q_i represents the immediate weighted cost of a criminal residing in community i committing a crime within the system during a single transition period.

Equation 2 implies that if criminals are allowed to commit offenses unrestrained by any outside agency, the cost of crime will approach an infinite value as n approaches infinity. This is not a realistic description of the actual environment within which the criminal acts. At the end of each time period, after an offense has been committed, the criminal is subject to the possibility of apprehension. The clearance ratio in community i, CR_i, is defined as the ratio of reported offenses cleared by arrests to the number of reported offenses, and represents the probability that a criminal committing a crime in i will be apprehended. Then, $1 - CR_i$ is the probability that the criminal will remain in the system after committing an offense in i. Incorporating this into the recurrent equation (2) yields:

$$TC_i(n) = q_i - \sum_{j=1}^{k} B_i \, a_{ij} \, TC_j(n-1) \qquad [3]$$

where: $i = 1, \ldots, k;$
$B_i = 1 - CR_i;$

and $TC_i(n)$ now represents the total expected cost of offenses generated by a criminal starting in community i adjusted by the probability that he or she will remain in the system after committing the offense.

To derive the total expected cost of crime generation per criminal in each community, over an infinite number of time periods, the set of equations in 3 must be solved simultaneously, resulting in:

$$TC = [I - BA]^{-1} \cdot q \qquad [4]$$

where TC is a kxl vector of unknown cost, q is a kxl intermediate weighted cost vector, B is a kxk diagonal matrix equal to $I - CR$ where I is a kxk identity matrix, and CR is a kxk diagonal matrix of CR's. A is a kxk Criminal Mobility Matrix (Fabrikant, 1975: 5).

The Policy Determination Step

The policy determination step provides for the solution of an optimal allocation of police manpower such that the total expected cost of criminal activity is minimized.[2] To achieve this, a criminal response function for each community i is defined by equation 5 as:

$$C_i = c_i(P_{ij}\,\overline{SE_i}) \qquad [5]$$

where: $i = 1, \ldots, k;$
C_i = the number of criminals in community i;
P_i = the number of police in i;

and SE_i expresses the socioeconomic conditions in i. It is expected that C_i will decrease as P_i increases, but at a decreasing rate, given no change in the socioeconomic conditions of the community. The policy determination step may now be written as:

$$\underset{P_i \in P}{\text{min}} \sum_{i=1}^{k} TC_i \cdot C_i \qquad [6]$$

subject to:
$$\sum_{i=1}^{k} P_i = \overline{P}, \text{ and } P_i > 0$$

where: $\overline{P}$ = the total number of police available for patrol functions in all districts; and

TC_i = the total expected cost associated with the offenses generated by a criminal residing in community i.

The solution of this minimization problem yields an optimal allocation of police over all communities.[3]

The Response Determination Step

Any given allocation of police patrols will result in corresponding responses by the criminal population. One response concerns direct effects on the size of the criminal population in each community as defined in the behavioral equation (5). Another possible outcome is the redistribution of criminals among communities. The dynamics of the redistribution is partially governed by the effectiveness of police to deter crime in their assigned communities as measured by the clearance ratio. If a new allocation of police results in altering its effectiveness, the distribution of offenses and thus the Criminal Mobility Matrix will be transformed accordingly. This can be represented by a two-stage process. The first stage relates the variation in the clearance ratio to the number of police patrols in i, and is represented by:

$$CR_i = CR_i (P_i) \qquad [7]$$

where i = 1, . . . k.

It is assumed that as policing is increased in community i, its effectiveness improves, causing CR to increase, but at a decreasing rate. Once the new CR is determined, the criminals' reactions to it are governed by:

$$A = f([CR]) \hspace{3cm} [8]$$

where $[A]$ = a k x k Criminal Mobility Matrix, and
$[CR]$ = a k x k clearance ratio matrix.

The Optimization Algorithm

Having specified the three major steps, the dynamic optimization procedure is as follows. The process starts by entering the initial conditions under the present police manpower allocation. These include the clearance ratios for each community (CR_i), the number of criminals in each community (C_i), the Criminal Mobility Matrix (A), and the expected immediate weighted costs (q_i). The probabilities of a criminal remaining in the system, B, are then derived. These serve as inputs to the determination of the expected costs per criminal in each community. The total expected cost for all communities is then determined and methods to reduce it via a superior police allocation are attempted. If no improvements are possible, the original police allocation instituted and the appropriate criminal responses are ascertained. As a result, new probabilities are calculated, followed by the determination of a new total expected cost. The testing procedure for improvement is again initiated and the system either terminates or continues to run until an optimal allocation is achieved.

THE EMPIRICAL IMPLEMENTATION OF THE MODEL

The Response Functions

The applicability of the model is dependent upon the validity and reliability of the estimated response functions in describing the actual behavior of criminal offenders and police patrols. Since there are numerous difficulties in obtaining accurate criminal data, the results derived from the estimation procedures must be interpreted with care. Unreported crime, variability in arrest rates, and the impossibility of actually measuring the number of criminals in each community may cause the estimated parameters of the response functions to be biased when using least-squares techniques. This does not necessarily negate the value of attempting to determine behavioral implications. In a recent study, Skogan (1974) evaluated the usefulness of criminal data and concluded that official statistics are not mere measurement artifacts but reflect real trends. Information derived from these statistics may properly be used for comparative or behavioral analysis.

Another difficulty in estimating the response functions is the possible feedback effects between police and criminals (Phillips et al., 1972). If feedback effects exist, single equation estimation of the response function and the police effectiveness function are subject to simultaneous equation bias. However, this system is conceived in terms of a recursive structure. That is, the allocation of patrols will first have a direct effect on the community clearance ratio, consequently altering the differentials of the clearance ratios between communities, and thus creating an incentive for criminals to readjust their choices of offense targets. Under this structure the single equation estimation technique is appropriate.

The final problem deals with the proper specification of the functional forms. It is difficult to determine, a priori, the exact functional forms which are theoretically correct and result in the best data fit. Furthermore, because of the small sample size and the lack of time series data on socioeconomic conditions, the inclusion of normalizing variables is greatly limited. To alleviate some of these problems, the time series data for the communities under study were pooled when reasonable assumptions could be made regarding the coefficients on the included variables.

A Description of the Data

The urban area selected for study is the city of Los Angeles. The choice was made on the basis of data availability, particularly with respect to data tracing criminals from their places of residence to their offense locations. This information is necessary to derive the Criminal Mobility Matrix and the corresponding redistribution of criminal activity resulting from the reallocation of police patrols. Unfortunately, data of this form were only available for juvenile arrestees. The type of crimes included in the data set were those that are amenable to economic analysis, mainly the property crimes of larceny, burglary, and robbery.

The sample area consisted of four inner communities defined as police districts by the Los Angeles Police Department: University, Hollenbeck, Wilshire, and 77th Street. These were chosen because of their relative boundary stability during the years 1956 through 1965. After 1965 there were some major boundary changes among districts, consequently eliminating the possibility of gathering comparable observations over time. All simulations regarding the allocation of police patrols are confined to the sample time period and districts.

To estimate the total potential number of juvenile criminals in each district, the arrest data is adjusted by the clearance ratio.[4] Since the only published data are average clearance ratios rather than clearance ratios specific to juvenile crimes, an upward bias in the estimated number of juvenile criminals in each district is expected.[5]

The normalizing variables that are estimated utilizing time series data are population and density. Time series data by district for other socioeconomic and demographic variables are not available. In the cross-sectional analysis of criminal mobility, additional socioeconomic variables are included.

The Criminal Response Function

The specific form of the criminal response function to be estimated, consistent with the economic implication of the model is:

$$C_i = a_i + b_i \frac{\lambda_i}{PAT_i} \qquad [9]$$

where C_i = the number of criminals, and PAT_i = the number of police in district i.[6] The variable λ_i is equal to $1/T$ where T is a linear decreasing sequence on numbers starting in 1956 and terminating in 1965. The inclusion of this variable adjusts for the possibility of changes over time in the environment of district i and techniques employed by the police which may cause shifts in the coefficient b. Since, at any given time period, λ is known, an accordingly adjusted b can be derived. This weighting scheme is used for all districts under investigation.

The incorporation of the variable λ_i in equation 9 introduces the problem of heteroscedasticity into the estimation procedure if Ordinary Least Squares (OLS) is used. To adjust for this difficulty, the data are transformed in order to conform to the Generalized Least Squares estimation approach. The adjusted equation now becomes:

$$PAT_i \cdot C_i = a_iPAT_i + b_i\lambda + e \qquad [10]$$

where e = normally distributed random error term with mean equal to zero and a constant variance.

The results of estimating equation 10 using OLS are presented in Table 7.1. In all districts the adjusted coefficients of determination are significant. The signs on all the b coefficients are as expected, positive and significant at the .01

TABLE 7.1   Estimation of the Criminal Response Function after Adjusting for Heteroscedasticity

PAT. C	PAT	λ	$\bar{R}^2$	F Test	Standard Error
University	943.52** (2.775)	725342* (4.605)	.786	29.41[+]	121,663
Hollenbeck	721.27* (7.032)	136442* (6.178)	.885	61.62[+]	16,693
Wilshire	472.21* (3.344)	473646* (7.565)	.917	88.89[+]	45,533
77th Street	708.68*** (1.860)	1178940* (6.234)	.893	66.48[+]	131,910

NOTE: t statistics are shown in parentheses below coefficient values.
*Significant at the .01 level (one-tail test); **significant at the .025 level (one-tail test); ***significant at the .05 level; + significant at the .01 level (two-tail test).

The Clearance Ratio Response Function

In estimating the clearance ratio response function, it has been assumed that the marginal effectiveness of police in terms of altering the clearance ratio is approximately the same in all districts after normalizing for differences in population and density. However, underlying conditions, independent of the level of police forces, might cause differences in the clearance ratios between districts. To incorporate this phenomenon into the estimated equation, a set of district dummy variables is included.

As in the previous analysis, a corresponding time weight is placed on the level of police forces to account for shifts in the marginal effectiveness of police over time. In this case the resulting heteroscedasticity is assumed to be minimal. The equation to be estimated is:

$$CR_{it} = \alpha_1 D_1 + \alpha_2 D_2 + \alpha_3 D_3 + \alpha_4 D_4 + \beta_1 POP_{it}$$
$$+ \beta_2 DEN_{it} + \beta_3(\lambda_t PAT_{it}) + \beta_4(\lambda_t PAT)2_{it} \qquad [11]$$

where: D_i = a set of district dummy variables (I = 1, 2, . . . , 4) such that when D_i = 1, then $D_i \neq j = 0$;
POP_{it} = the population in district i in time period t;
DEN_{it} = the population density in district i in time period t; and
λ_t = the time corresponding weight defined previously.

The results of estimating equation 11 using ordinary least squares are:

$$CR_{it} = -.919D_1 - .582D_2 - 1.245D_3 - .939D_4 + .0000038POP_{it}\text{***}$$
$$\quad (-.825) \quad (-.630) \quad (-1.053) \quad (-9.39) \quad\quad (1.827)$$

$$+ .0000DEN_{it} + .000437\lambda_t PAT_{it}\text{*} - .000000239(\lambda_t PAT_{it})^2\text{**}$$
$$\quad (.354) \quad\quad (2.62) \quad\quad\quad (-2.28)$$

$$R^{-2} = .423 \qquad F = 3.35 \qquad S.E. = .0891$$

t statistics are shown in parentheses below the coefficient values.
    *Significant at .01 level (one-tail test).
   **Significant at .025 level (one-tail test).
  ***Significant at .1 level (two-tail test).

Although the adjusted R^{-2} is fairly low, the equation is significant at the .01 level. As assumed, an analysis of the residuals does not suggest the existence of heteroscedasticity.

None of the intercept terms prove to be different from zero, nor are the disparities between them significant. The normalizing variables POP_{it} and DEN_{it} are also insignificant at a greater than .05 level. This is partially explained by the collinearity between them.[7] The coefficients critical to the model on the variables $\lambda_t PAT_{it}$ and $(\lambda_t PAT_{it})^2$ exhibit the correct sign and are both statistically significant.

Economic interpretation of the quadratic equation (11) requires that the relevant section of the parabola be the upward sloping portion. To show that the system operates on the relevant portion, the maximum point of the function is derived for 1965. The number of patrols consistent with this point is 914, 40 patrolmen over the total number actually allocated to all four districts in the sample.

The Criminal Reaction Function

To derive the criminal reaction function, the data set is expanded to include all 17 major police reporting districts in Los Angeles. It is to these districts that the Los Angeles Police Department allocated its police. From the data gathered in each district, a Criminal Flow Matrix is constructed by tracing juvenile criminals from the districts in which they reside to the districts in which they commit their offenses.

The criminal reaction function is derived using a behavioral model based on the economic theory of choice. Incorporated in the model are the economic and control factors which encourage or inhibit criminal spillovers among communities (Fabrikant, 1979). It is specified as:

$$O_{ij}/O_i = a \cdot ADIJ^{\gamma_1} \cdot VOOHIJ^{\gamma_2} \cdot CRIJ^{\gamma_3}$$
$$\cdot PCFIJ^{\gamma_4} \cdot e \qquad [12]$$

where: O_{ij} = the conditional probability of a juvenile criminal coming from district i and committing property crimes in district j;

ADIJ = an adjusted distance variable between the geographic centers of each district. It is a proxy variable for the direct out-of-pocket costs to the juvenile for committing an offense.

VOOHIJ = a comparative measure of the average median value of owner-occupied housing in the target district j with that of the criminal's resident district i. It is a proxy variable for the comparative expected gain or opportunities of committing a crime in a specific district.

CRIJ = a comparative measure of the clearance ratios between the target district j and the criminal's resident district i. It represents the relative probability of apprehension and is directly related to the allocation of police patrols.

PCFIJ = a measure of the potential criminal flows from district i to j and the competition in j. It is an indicator of the juvenile's willingness to revise his allocation of offenses, should there be a change in the relative competitive positions between districts i and j.

e = the error term assumed to be normally distributed with a constant variance.

In accordance with the theoretical model, it is expected that:

$$\gamma_1 < 0, \gamma_2 > 0, \gamma_3 < 0, \text{ and } \gamma_4 > 0.$$

The results of estimating this equation utilizing OLS are:

$$\ln(0_{ij}/0_i = -3.47 - 2.39\ln\text{ADIJ}^* + 1.48\ln\text{VOOHIJ}^* - .83\ln\text{CRIJ}^{**}$$
$$(-2.37)(-15.36)(4.36)(-1.64)$$

$$+ .29\ 1n\text{PCFIJ}^{**}$$
$$(1.80)$$

$$R^{-2} = .51 \qquad \text{and } f_{4,251} = 65.8$$

t statistics are shown in parentheses below coefficient values.
*Significant at the .005 level (one-tail test).
**Significant at the .05 level (one-tail test).

All the signs on the regressors are consistent with the theoretical behavioral implications. The adjusted coefficient of determination (R^{-2}) is significant, implying that 51 percent of the variation in the probability that a criminal in district i will commit his or her next offense in j is explained. The distance variable, representing the costs to the juveniles, and the opportunities variable are significant at the .005 level; while the competitive index variable is significant at the .05 level. The clearance ratio or the law enforcement control variable is significant at the .05 level. This result supports the proposition that juvenile criminals do respond to the effectiveness of police patrols in the various districts. Consequently, if there is a reallocation of these patrols, a new distribution of offense activity is likely.

SIMULATION OF THE POLICE
ALLOCATION OPTIMIZATION PROCEDURE

To initialize the optimization procedure, the estimated number of criminals and the clearance ratios for each of the four districts are determined under the actual police allocation for 1965. The remaining districts are aggregated into a single dummy district, and the estimated number of criminals as well as the weighted average clearance ratios are derived. Socioeconomic conditions in the aggregate district and the number of police patrols assigned to it are held constant during the simulation. The rationale for including the aggregate district is to close the system, thus assuring that the Criminal Mobility Matrix is consistent with the theoretical structure. Note that this assumption restricts the analysis to a partial equilibrium framework.

The average cost per property crime is calculated for all sample districts and for the aggregate district. An adjusted Criminal Mobility Matrix based on the clearance ratios for 1965 is then derived. From this the expected immediate cost per criminal by district is calculated. The entire set of initial conditions is presented in Table 7.2.

After a preliminary test of the program, the optimization procedure is implemented using the actual data for the year 1965.[8] The results are presented in Table 7.3. As will be observed in Table 7.3, under iteration I, the system converges after the second iteration, resulting in an allocation significantly different than the one in existence during 1965. The total discounted cost is reduced by $338,415 and the total number of criminals generated by 174. Major decreases in the generation of criminals take place in the University and 77th Street districts, both of which are characterized by high crime rates. Note also that because the clearance ratio in the University district has increased relative to that of the other districts, an increase in the probability of criminals leaving the University district is expected. This shift is observed in the new Criminal Mobility Matrix. In contrast, the clearance ratio in the Wilshire district has declined relative to that of other districts, resulting in a 4.3 percent increase in the probability that criminals in the Wilshire district will commit their next crimes in that same district, excluding the aggregate district.

In order to compare the results under the condition of criminal mobility with that of confining criminals to committing offenses in their own districts, it is necessary to change the Criminal Mobility Matrix to an identity matrix. This implies that the probability of a criminal committing an offense in a district other than the one in which he or she now operates is equal to zero. The results of incorporating the identity matrix into the optimization procedure are presented in Table 7.4. Observe that the initial total expected cost of criminal activity in the static model is $860,699 less than in the mobility model. This is caused by forcing the criminals to commit offenses exclusively in their own districts, rather than allowing them to seek districts which yield higher expected returns. After the optimization procedure, a new allocation of police is derived which differs significantly from the one in existence in 1965. When compared to the allocation under the mobility case, the direction of the changes for each district from the original allocation appears to be the same, while the magnitudes differ by varying degrees.

It is interesting to observe that while the total expected cost under the optimal allocation in the static case is less than that in the mobility case, the total number of criminals expected to be deterred is also less. It is concluded from

TABLE 7.2 Initializing Conditions for the Optimization Simulation

	Estimated Number of Juvenile Criminals[a]	Weighted Average Clearance Ratio[b]	Number of Police	Average Weighted Cost per Offense Index	Expected Cost per Criminal
University	4448	.167	207	$224.70	$235.31
Hollenbeck	2046	.166	103	132.76	161.89
Wilshire	2665	.142	216	243.71	244.69
77th Street	5463	.196	248	335.00	318.73
All Other	14389	.160	1559	235.70	254.80
TOTAL	29011		2333		

SOURCE: Data from Los Angeles Police Department *Statistical Digest* (1965).

a. Rounded to the nearest whole number.

b. Rounded to three decimal places.

TABLE 7.3   Tabulated Results for the Mobility Case of the Optimization Procedure

	Initial Conditions					First Iteration					Second Iteration				
	#2	#3	#4	#5	#6	#7	#8	#9[a]	#10	#11	#12	#13[b]	#14	#15	#16
University	4448	.167	207	1519.5	6,758,736	4266	.171	218	1516.9	6,471,095	4421	.168	209	1529.7	6,762,804
Hollenbeck	2046	.166	103	1300.5	2,660,823	2279	.160	88	1322.9	3,014,889	1827	.174	123	1276.7	2,322,531
Wilshire	2665	.142	216	1627.6	4,337,554	3066	.131	183	1682.1	5,157,319	2830	.137	201	1656.7	4,688,461
77th Street	5463	.196	248	1599.8	8,739,707	4837	.207	285	1549.7	7,492,513	5598	.194	241	1618.5	9,060,363
All Other	14389	.160	1559	1575.9	22,675,625	14389	.160	1559	1573.3	22,638,214	14389	.160	1559	1580.6	22,743,253
TOTAL	29011		2333		45,172,445	28837		2333		44,784,030	29065		2333		45,587,412

NOTE: #2 = number of juvenile criminals; #3 = clearance ratio; #4 = number of police; #5 = discounted SC per juvenile in dollars; #6 = total discounted SC in dollars; #7 = number of juvenile criminals; #8 = clearance ratio; #9 = number of police[a]; #10 = discounted SC per juvenile in dollars; #11 = total discount SC in dollars; #12 = number of juvenile criminals; #13 = clearance ratio[b]; #14 = number of police; #15 = discounted SC per juvenile in dollars; #16 = total discounted SC in dollars.
a. Rounded to the nearest whole number.
b. Rounded to three decimal places.

TABLE 7.4 Tabulated Results for the Static Case of the Optimization Procedures

	#2	#3[b]	#4	#5	#6	#7	#8[b]	#9[a]	#10	#11
University	4448	.167	207	1,345.5	5,984,784	4396	.168	210	1337.5	5,879,650
Hollenbeck	2046	.166	103	798.8	1,634,345	2665	.153	70	867.7	2,312,447
Wilshire	2665	.142	216	1,776.3	4,573,939	2943	.134	192	1818.7	5,352,434
77th Street	5463	.196	248	1,712.9	9,346,647	4612	.212	302	1580.2	7,287,882
All Other	14389	.160	1559	1,582.6	22,772,031	14389	.160	1559	1582.6	22,772,031
TOTAL	29011		2333		44,311,746	29005		2333		43,604,444

NOTE: #2 = number of juvenile criminals; #3 = clearance ratio[b]; #4 = number of police; #5 = discounted SC per juvenile in dollars; #6 = total discounted SC in dollars; #7 = number of juvenile criminals; #8 = clearance ratio[b]; #9 = number of police[a]; #10 = discounted SC per juvenile in dollars; #11 = total district SC in dollars.
a. Rounded to the nearest whole number
b. Rounded to three decimal places

this that by incorporating the existence of spillovers, a more efficient allocation of patrols will be achieved with respect to the reduction of the total number of criminals.

SUMMARY AND CONCLUSIONS

The optimization procedure presented in this study is but one method which may be used to incorporate externalities when allocating public or private goods among distinct geographic areas. The methodology employed conserves on data requirements and affords the greatest flexibility in specifying criminal and law enforcement behavioral relationships. The results of the simulation clearly indicate that without the internalization of criminal spillovers a nonoptimal allocation of police patrols will result.

NOTES

1. At the time this study was carried out, the Los Angeles Police Department used a police allocation formulation which incorporated such decision variables as the number of offenses and the total dollar value of property stolen in each district. The police allocation formula was updated every 3 to 6 months.

For complete information on the Los Angeles Police Department's methodology, see Los Angeles Police Department, Patrol Bureau Memorandum No. 10 (November 3, 1968).

2. It is not necessary to confine the objective to the minimization of the total discounted cost of criminal activity. Other objectives, such as the minimization of the total number of criminals in the urban area, can be easily incorporated in the simulation.

3. The solution to equation 5 is achieved by forming the Lagrangian, substituting equation 5 into equation 6, and then solving for the first-order conditions. This yields a set of $k + 1$ equations with $k + 1$ unknowns. Solving this set of equations simultaneously yields an optimal allocation of P_is. The second-order conditions for the existence of a minimum are assured through the assumptions on equation 5. Furthermore, corner solutions are eliminated by the second constraint in equation 6, assuring a positive number of police patrols in each district.

4. The estimate of total juvenile offenses was derived using the following formula:

Juvenile offenses = juvenile arrests/(total arrests/total offenses)

This is practically identical to the one used by Phillips et al. (1972: 496).

5. Since the majority of juvenile criminals committed their crimes in the same district in which they resided, the clearance ratio used was the one determined for that particular district. However, the clearance ratio, which takes into account all offenders, may not necessarily be an appropriate representation of the juvenile clearance ratio. Indeed, as Phillips et al. (1972) point out,

$$\text{Juvenile Clearance Ratio} = k \cdot \frac{\text{Total Arrests}}{\text{Total Offenses}}$$

where k in this case is most likely greater than one. Support for this assertion is found in the President's Commission on Law Enforcement and the Administration of Justice (1967: 55).

6. Numerous empirical studies have been carried out on the determination of offense generation function and law enforcement production functions. In all of these studies the concentration has been on the generation of offenses rather than criminals, the assumption being that in any given area there is a direct correspondence between the number of criminals and offenses. To a certain degree this is true, particularly when dealing with large geographic area. However, when analyzing the districts in an urban area, this assumption may not hold, especially if there are considerable amounts of criminal spillovers. It is for this reason that a different approach was used in this study.

Some of the more recent empirical studies are by Chapman (1976), Ehrlich (1973), Giertz (1970), Mehay (1973), Phillips and Votey (1974), Phillips et al. (1973), Sjoquest (1973), and Votey and Phillips (1972).

7. A test for colinearity between DEN and POP was carried out by estimating the relationship between the two using OLS. Again the data were pooled resulting in the following estimated expression:

$$DEN = 15744.7D_1{}^* + 13715.7D_2{}^* + 15989.0D_3{}^* + 13373.2D_4{}^* - 112202.0POP^{**}$$
$$(13.94) \qquad (23.92) \qquad (9.93) \qquad (9.55) \qquad (-1.76)$$

$$R^{-2} = .9363 \qquad 4^F35 = 128.54 \qquad S.E. = 297.5$$

t statistics are shown in parentheses below coefficient values.
 *Significant at the .005 level (two-tail test).
**Significant at the .05 level (one-tail test).

The results confirm the relationship between DEN and POP.

8. Preliminary tests on hypothetical data for a simple two-district model were run to determine the convergence properties of the optimization procedure. It was found that in almost every case not more than four iterations were necessary to reach an optimal allocation of police such that the total expected costs of criminal activity were at a minimum. It was also observed that the total expected costs were fairly responsive to the clearance ratio, consequently affecting the police allocation. On the other hand, marginal changes in criminal movement among districts, as represented by the a_{ij} in the Criminal Mobility Matrix, did not affect the alloca-

tion of police significantly, as did the changes in the total expected costs assigned to each district.

REFERENCES

BECKER, G. S. (1968) "Crime and punishment: an economic approach." Journal of Political Economy 76, 2: 169-217.

CHAPMAN, J. I. (1976) "An economic model of crime and police: some empirical results." Journal of Research in Crime and Delinquency 13, 1: 48-63.

EHRLICH, I. (1973) "Participation in illegitimate activities: a theoretical and empirical investigation." Journal of Political Economy 81, 3: 521-565.

FABRIKANT, R. (1979) "The distribution of criminal offenses in an urban environment: a spatial analysis of criminal spillovers and of juvenile offenders." American Journal of Economics and Sociology 38, 1: 31-47.

_____ (1977) "A long overdue comment on Shoup's standards for distributing a free government service: crime prevention." Public Finance/Finances Publiques (January): 111-118.

_____ (1975) "The allocation of public good in the presence of spillovers: a case study in law enforcement." Ph.D. dissertation, University of California—Santa Barbara.

GIERTZ, F. J. (1970) An Economic Analysis of the Distribution of Police Patrol Forces. Springfield, VA: National Technical Information Service.

HAKIM, S. (1980) "The attraction of property crimes to suburban localities: a revised economic model." Urban Studies 17, 3: 265-276.

_____ A. OVADIA, E. SAGI, and J. WEINBLATT (1979) "Interjurisdictional spillovers of crime and police expenditures." Land Economics 55, 2: 200-212.

HOWARD, R. (1960) Dynamic Programming and Markov Processes. Cambridge: MIT Press.

Los Angeles Police Department (1956-1973) Statistical Digest. Los Angeles: Author.

MEHAY, S. L. (1977) "Interjurisdictional spillovers of urban police services." Southern Economic Journal 43, 3: 1352-1359.

_____ (1973) "Production functions for crime-deterrent police services." Ph.D. dissertation, University of California—Los Angeles.

OZENNE, T. O. (1972) "The economics of theft and security choice." Ph.D. dissertation, University of California—Los Angeles.

PHILLIPS, L. and H. L. VOTEY, Jr. (1974) "An economic model for optimal allocation of LEAA funds in California." University of California—Santa Barbara. (unpublished)

_____ and J. HOWELL (1976) "Handguns and homicide: minimizing losses and the cost of control." Journal of Legal Studies 5, 2: 463-480.

PHILLIPS, L., H. L. VOTEY, Jr., and D. MAXWELL (1972) "Crime, youth, and the labor market." Journal of Political Economy 80: 491-503.

President's Commission on Law Enforcement and the Administration of Justice (1967) The Challenge of Crime in a Free Society. Washington, DC: Government Printing Office.

PRESS, J.S. (1971) Some Effects of an Increase in Police Manpower in the 20th Precinct of New York City. New York: Rand Institute.

ROTTENBERG, S. (1970) "The social cost of crime and crime prevention," pp. 43-58 in B. N. McLennan (ed.) Crime in Urban Society. New York: Dunellen.

SJOQUIST, D. L. (1973) "Property crime and economic behavior: some empirical results." American Economic Review 63, 3: 439-446.

SKOGAN, W. G. (1974) "The validity of official crime statistics: an empirical investigation." Social Science Quarterly 55 (June): 25-38.

STIGLER, G. J. (1970) "The optimum enforcement of laws." Journal of Political Economy 78 (May/June): 526-534.

THEIL, H. (1971) Principles of Econometrics. New York: John Wiley.

TULLOCK, G. (1968) "An economic approach to crime." Social Science Quarterly 50, 1: 59-71.

VOTEY, H. L., Jr., and L. PHILLIPS (1972) "Police effectiveness and the production function of law enforcement." Journal of Legal Studies 1, 2: 423-435.

8

Martin T. Katzman
University of Texas—Dallas

THE SUPPLY OF CRIMINALS
A Geo-Economic Examination

Two long-standing generalizations about the geography of crime are that crime rates are proportional to city size and that, within cities, crime rates are higher in neighborhoods of lower socioeconomic status (Hoch, 1972; Harries, 1974). A recent analysis of residential mobility (Katzman, 1980) indicates that in their choice of destination, movers are sensitive to interneighborhood differences in crime rates. Families with children and with high incomes are particularly prone to avoid high-crime neighborhoods. While patterns of residential mobility are strongly influenced by job location and physical housing quality, relatively low crime rates may contribute to suburbanization and the recent disproportional growth of smaller towns and cities.

Movement to a safe neighborhood may reduce the chance of victimization, but crime rates appear to be increasing in the suburbs and small towns as well (Hakim et al., 1979). While conclusive time series data are unavailable, there has been an apparent leveling of social class and geographic disparities in the incidence of victimization. This democratization may reflect: the movement of the lower class to the suburbs, increasing mobility of the crime-prone population, and the adoption of certain aspects of the criminal lifestyle by members of the middle class. Let us consider each in turn.

First, while more affluent groups have historically paved the way to the suburbs and exurbs, lower-income groups have been participating in the suburbanization process for several decades. While a large proportion of the white poor has lived in the suburbs since the 1960s (Kain, 1969: Table 3), blacks have begun a massive move to the suburbs since the late 1970s (Katzman, 1980). As illustrated by the model of housing "filtration," newer housing is constructed for more affluent families, who sell their current housing to members of income groups one rung below. All groups improve their physical housing by this process, while neighborhoods appear to decline in social class. Thus social classes which produce a disproportion of perpetrators of violent and property crimes are becoming suburban to a greater extent.

Second, higher-income groups are finding it more and more difficult to preserve their physical[1] and social distance from lower-income groups by residential mobility. This is because of the increasing geographical mobility of potential criminals, with the near universal spread of automobile ownership and the completion of radial and circumferential freeways.

Third, the "drug culture," formerly confined to criminal elements, has diffused from the lower class to the middle class, particularly the youth. Teenagers commit a disproportionate share of crimes at any rate, and the spread of behavior that is illegal per se (the use of narcotics) may induce other illegal behavior (thefts to support a drug habit).

Most studies of the ecology of crime relate neighborhood crime rates to the characteristics of its residents. These ecological correlations are quite high indeed. For example, in the 44 Dallas County communities examined below, violent crime rates displayed the following bivariate correlations: r = +.61 with percentage black; r = −.54 with percentage males white-collar; r = −.51 with percentage completing high school; and r = −.45 with median income. One could thus avoid crime by moving into a neighborhood that was safe, as indicated by its socioeconomic composition. The suburbanization of the lower class, increases in geographic mobility, and the spread of lower-class culture among the middle class make finding a safe neighborhood increasingly difficult. Presumably, the safety of a neighborhood varies inversely with the proportion of criminals residing in its midst and with its accessibility to potential criminals from elsewhere.

This hypothesis is consistent with the burgeoning literature on the rational criminal. Here criminal behavior is viewed as a rational choice of alternative courses of legitimate and illegitimate action, with their associated costs and benefits. The objective of crimes like burglary, robbery, larceny, and perhaps auto theft, is clearly the appropriation of property. Areas of great wealth, like commercial districts and high-income neighborhoods, would be obvious targets. The expected value of criminal action depends upon the probability of success as well as the worth of the potential booty. This probability in turn is reduced by policing, neighborhood vigilance, and self-protection on the part of the intended victims (Clotfelter, 1977, 1978). Such protective measures, in turn, depend upon the likelihood of victimization. Finally, the costs of crime are expressed as the expected value of punishment. This value is a function of the likelihood of being apprehended, prosecuted, and convicted, and the severity of the punishment. The likelihood of being caught varies directly with police expenditure (Hakim et al., 1979).

Neglected in this literature is a cost that plays a key role in understanding metropolitan development: commuting, or the time and money costs of "journey to crime." Because of these costs, criminals are more likely to commit crimes closer to home. Capone and Nichols (1975) found that in Miami one-third of the offenders apprehended committed offenses within one mile of their own homes; three-quarters, within four miles. Smith (1976) found that in Rochester half of the apprehended offenders committed crimes within two miles of their own homes. Juvenile offenders tend to be more parochial than adult offenders. One-third of juveniles apprehended in Philadelphia committed offenses within one-quarter mile of home; three-quarters, within one mile of home (Turner, 1969).

Journey to crime apparently displays the distance-decay characteristics of most human spatial interaction, from shopping trips to interregional trade (Katzman, 1977). As predictable from the rational criminal model, the rate of distance-decay varies inversely with the value of the potential booty at the destination, measured as the mean value of business premises (Capone and Nichols, 1975).

The distance-decay phenomenon suggests placing the analysis of crime within a "potential model." The supply of criminals to a given neighborhood j is a weighted sum of the number of criminals with access to that neighborhood. The weights reflect the distance between the origin of the criminal, neighborhood i, and destination j. The following equation expresses the supply of criminals to each neighborhood j (S_j) as:

$$S_j = \sum_i K_i / d_{ij}^{\alpha} \qquad [1]$$

where: $K_i =$ the number of potential criminals in neighborhood i;

  $d_{ij} =$ the distance between origin i and destination j; and

  $\alpha =$ the distance-decay coefficient.

Potentials calculated like those above have been used to predict the intensity of demand for a given location, particularly for shopping centers (Isard, 1960).

Violent crimes are difficult to place into a framework of the rational criminal. A large share of violent crime is inflicted among relatives, friends, and acquaintances. The motivations for such "crimes of passion," are not readily amenable to economic analysis. As noted by Boggs (1966), the spatial distribution of offenses and offenders are nearly congruent for violent crimes, while the distribution of offenses and offenders differs markedly for property crimes.

Not surprisingly, violent crime rates are more highly correlated with neighborhood social class than property crime rates. For the 44 Dallas County communities, serious property crime displays the following bivariate correlations with a neighborhood's own socioeconomic characteristics: $r = +.39$ with percentage black; $r = -.31$ with percentage males white-collar; $r = -.31$ with percentage completing high school; and $r = -.17$ with median income. These correlations are more than 20 points lower than those for violent crime, listed above: $+.61$, $-.54$, $-.51$, and $-.45$, respectively. These comparisons suggest that the distance-decay gradient is steeper for violent crimes than for property crimes.

There are several difficulties in operationalizing the concept of "crime potential." First, to what geographical origins, i, should potential criminals be assigned? Second, how are potential criminals, K, to be identified? Third, what is the appropriate distance-decay coefficient? Fourth, how is distance to be measured?

While people spend their sleeping hours at home, they may travel outside their neighborhoods several times each week to work, to shop, to attend school, to recreate, or just to loiter. Opportunities to profit from criminals acts may arise during any of these trips. Neighborhood of origin is actually a probabilistic concept, which is reflected in a time-location budget. In the absence of detailed time budgeting, the location of neighborhood of residence serves as a measure of central tendency.

Potential criminals may be viewed as being randomly derived from the following populations: the total population, the poor population, or the teenage population. The distance-decay parameter, α, has been estimated in the range of .75-2.5 (Harries, 1974; Capone and Nichols, 1975; Rengert, 1977). As suggested above, teenagers may be less mobile than the population as a whole, as represented by a higher decay coefficient. In the absence of firmer knowledge, experiments with alternative coefficients of .75, 1.0, 1.5 and 2.0 are used for the three populations.

Distance between neighborhoods should be measured by time and money costs between their centers. In a metropolitan area with a well-developed transportation network, airline distances are a fairly good approximation for these costs. Because cities differ in time and space in the quality of their transportation networks, the coefficient of airline distance is unlikely to remain invariant. Prior to the nearly universal diffusion of access to the automobile, the coefficient of airline distance was undoubtedly lower than today.[2] Fragmentary evidence (Rengert, 1977; Capone and Nichols, 1975) indicates that cities such as Philadelphia, whose major development predated the automobile, display higher coefficients than auto-age cities such as Miami: 2.5 versus 1.5.

EMPIRICAL ANALYSIS

The effect of the supply potential of criminals on neighborhood crime rates is tested for the city of Dallas, Texas, in 1970. Neighborhoods are defined as 27 homogeneous "Statistical Community Areas," as delineated by the city planning department. The criminal supply area obviously does not stop at city boundaries. Potentials are calculated by including the population in 17 additional communities which make up suburban and unincorporated Dallas County. These suburban communities are delineated by school district lines. Since Dallas County included about 85 percent of the population in the Dallas Standard Metropolitan Statistical Area of 1970, the 44 county communities come close to including the entire criminal population that may victimize residents of the city of Dallas. Potentials are underestimated for the suburban communities on the periphery of the county, which may attract criminals from adjacent counties. For this reason, suburban communities are excluded from the final regression analysis.

The following variables for each community are computed by aggregating 1970 census tract data: total population, population age 14-19, number of poor families, and median housing value. Where tracts are split by community boundaries, tract population is allocated in rough proportion to the area in each community. The average community has 10,000 families, or 30,000 population.

Distances among the 44 communities of origin are calculated from the apparent population centers of each. These centers are visually estimated by the density of streets on a census map. The potentials for the 27 city communities are computed with the four alternate distance coefficients and then divided by the community's own population. This standardization procedure expresses potentials on the same per capita basis as the crime rates are normally reported. It should be noted that a neighborhood's own population is excluded from the potential calculation. The effect of a neighborhood's own characteristics on its crime rate is determined separately.

The 1970 crime rates are reported at the level of 101 city police beats. The beats are aggregated and apportioned among the 27 city neighborhoods. Rates are calculated separately for major property crimes (burglary, larceny, robbery, and auto theft) and violent crimes (homicide, rape, aggravated assault). In 1970 the mean rates of property and violent crime were 60 per thousand and 6 per thousand, respectively.

Boggs (1966) notes that resident population may be an inadequate and misleading denominator for computing crime rates. Business districts are populated by large daytime populations and have enormous property wealth per acre. Dividing the incidence of crime by the small resident population overstates the likelihood of victimization. Hakim et al. (1979) measure crime per acre as an alternative. Dividing crime by the resident population does provide a fairly good indicator of the proability of victimization within one's neighborhood. For this reason, crime rates are expressed here on the conventional per population basis.

As a first approximation, crime rates are correlated with potentials for the three population groups, using the four alternate distance-decay coefficients (Table 8.1). The pattern of bivariate correlations for the entire county and for the city alone are quite similar. Several interesting relationships can be seen in either pattern.

First, the correlations are invariably higher for the larger alphas, the distance-decay coefficients. This corroborates the hypothesized sensitivity of neighborhood crime rates to the characteristics of the more accessible neighboring communities.

Second, the crime rate in a neighborhood is unrelated to its accessibility to teenagers. This finding is inconsistent with the hypothesized propensity of teenagers to commit a disproportion of property crimes.

Third, the crime rate in a neighborhood is more closely related to its accessibility to the poor than to the total population. This finding is consistent with the literature on the rational criminal, in that the poor have relatively low opportunity costs for their time.

Fourth, the property crime rate of a neighborhood is more closely related to "poverty potentials" than to its local percentage of poor. In other words, the characteristics of a

TABLE 8.1   Bivariate Correlations of Neighborhood Crime Rates with Population Potentials and Own Characteristics: Dallas, 1970

Characteristic	City, n = 27		County, n = 44	
	Property	Violent	Property	Violent
Median housing value	−.27	−.47*	−.25*	−.42*
Teenagers/p.c.				
Alpha = .75	.06	.02	.08	.09
Alpha = 1.0	.07	.03	.09	.10
Alpha = 1.5	.08	.04	.11	.12
Alpha = 2.0	.09	.04	.11	.12
Own	−.09	−.03	−.08	.02
Poor/p.c.				
Alpha = .75	.14	.09	.16	.16
Alpha = 1.0	.20	.14	.21	.22
Alpha = 1.5	.32*	.24	.32*	.33*
Alpha = 2.0	.44*	.35*	.42*	.42*
Own	.13	.42*	.13	.49*
Total population/p.c.				
Alpha = .75	.08	.04	.10	.11
Alpha = 1.0	.11	.06	.13	.13
Alpha = 1.5	.17	.11	.19	.19
Alpha = 2.0	.24	.17	.25*	.25*

*Significance = .05.

neighborhood's local population are a worse predictor of likelihood of its residents' property being stolen than are the characteristics of surrounding neighborhoods. This finding would appear to contradict the hypothesis of criminal rationality because the local poor would appear to have cheaper access to local property than the poor of surrounding neighborhoods. However, there are several hidden costs of committing property crimes in one's own neighborhood. One cost would simply be the psychological cost of violating norms against the calculated victimization of friends and neighbors, members of the in-group. There would be less moral restraint against victimizing strangers, members of the out-group. Perhaps more important, one is more likely to be recognized, and hence apprehended, in committing a crime on the home turf.

Fifth, violent crime rates are more closely related to the neighborhood's local percentage of poor than to "poverty potentials." This finding is consistent with the view of violent crime as largely a crime of passion, committed among individuals in frequent contact.

Sixth, the bivariate correlation between median housing value and crime rates is negative. This common finding (see Boggs, 1966) reflects the confounding of supply and demand factors: High-income individuals are less likely to commit crimes, but they have more to steal.

Regression analysis provides a way of extricating the various demographic effects on crime. The correlations among the various potential measures themselves are extremely high, generally greater than .9. This means that utilizing several of these measures in any regression would pose great problems in multicollinearity. The correlations between a neighborhood's local poor and the various potential measures are somewhat lower (about $+.6$), which poses lesser problems of multicollinearity. Median housing value is insignificantly correlated with any of the potential measures, although as expected it is correlated with a neighborhood's local poverty ($r = -.47$).

Several regressions of property and violent crime rates in the city of Dallas are performed. Numbered 1 to 10, each

column in Tables 8.2 and 8.3 represents a different specification. In all of the regressions, neighborhood median housing value is included, but the demographic variables differ.

Standardized regression coefficients (betas) are reported
because the raw coefficients of the potentials are not readily
interpretable. The beta coefficient indicates by how many
standard deviations the dependent variable changes when
an independent variable changes by one standard deviation. The magnitude of the beta also provides a useful indicator of a variable's unique contribution to the explained
variance. The standard deviations and variances of all variables are, of course, specific to the sample under consideration, that is, neighborhoods in Dallas. The measures of
goodness-of-fit are the adjusted coefficient of determination (R^2), the F-ratio, and the standard error of the estimate.
The standard error of the estimate is expressed as the raw
standard error of estimate divided by the standard deviation of the dependent variable.

The results for property crime are considered first (Table
8.2). As suggested by the bivariate correlations, property
crime rates are not highly related to a neighborhood's local
proportion poor or teenaged (columns 1-3). Property crime
rates are, however, better related to "poverty potential"
(columns 4-5). "Teenage potential" and "total population
potential" have little impact on property crime (columns
6-8). In all of these regressions, median housing value has
the wrong sign, because of the confounded meaning of this
variable. Probably the unmeasured social class (the supply
of criminals) embodied in this variable outweighs the housing as an indicator of appropriable booty (the demand side).

The best fitting regressions include two potentials
(columns 9-10). When either teenage potential or total population potential are held constant, property crime is positively related to neighborhood housing value, its local proportion of poor families, and its poverty potential. These
variables all have the correct sign. These coefficients, as
well as the overall relationship, are highly significant.

TABLE 8.2 Influences on Property Crime, Dallas, 1970: Beta Coefficients.

Independent Variable	Regression Specification									
	1	2	3	4	5	6	7	8	9	10
Median housing value	-.27*	-.27*	-.17	-.20*	-.36*	-.27*	-.26*	-.26*	.29*	.44*
Poor families/p.c.										
Local	.01		.21		.44*				.26*	.26*
Alpha = 2.0				.40*	.65*				2.40*	4.24*
Teenagers/p.c.										
Local							-.57*			
Alpha = 2.0			-.23				.57*		-2.27*	-4.0*
Total population/p.c.										
Alpha = 2.0						-.08		.23	.80*	.79
R^2	.04	.05	.02	.20*	.26*	.08	.10	.09	.43	.43
F	.98	1.06	.82	3.58*	3.67*	1.08	1.61	1.73	24.00*	23.76*
Standardized s.e.e.	.96	.96	.95	.88	.82	.96	.91	.93	.43	.43

*Significance = .05.

The best property crime regressions can be stated rather simply. When the accessibility of a neighborhood to the entire surrounding population (or the teenage population) is held constant, its property crime rate rises with its wealth, its proportion of poor, and with its accessibility to the surrounding poor. Neighborhoods in which the median housing value is one standard deviation above the mean have property crime rates .29 to .44 standard deviations above the mean, holding other factors constant. Neighborhoods in which the proportion of poor is one standard deviation above the mean have property crime rates about .26 standard deviations above the mean. Neighborhoods in which accessibility to the surrounding poor is one standard deviation above the mean have property crime rates 2 to 4 standard deviations above the mean. In other words, variations in property crime rates are far more sensitive to neighborhood accessibility to the surrounding poor than to the local proportion of poor or to local housing values.

The regressions for violent crime display a tighter fit with local characteristics than regressions for property crime (Table 8.3). Like the property crime regressions, the best specifications for violent crime include median housing values, local proportion of poor, and accessibility to the surrounding poor. The beta coefficients for housing values and poverty potentials are almost identical to those in the best property crime equations. The beta values for local proportion poor are substantially higher in the violent crime equation, .85 versus .26 in the property crime equation. In other words, as indicated by the bivariate correlations, violent crime rates are more closely related to the characteristics of a neighborhood's population than is property crime rate.

CONCLUSION

The analysis of Dallas provides modest support for the notion that the accessibility of a neighborhood to prospective criminals influences its crime rate. While a neighborhood's local demographic composition provides a good

TABLE 8.3 Influences on Violent Crime, Dallas, 1970: Beta Coefficients.

Independent Variable	Regression Specification									
	1	2	3	4	5	6	7	8	9	10
Median housing value	-.35*	-.47*	-.14*	-.42*	-.37*	-.47*	-.47*	-.46*	.30*	.45*
Poor families/p.c.										
Local	.27		.70*		.13				.86*	.85*
Alpha = 2.0				.27*	.20				2.03*	3.90*
Teenagers/p.c.										
Local		-.02	-.50*				-.20			
Alpha = 2.0						.04	.21			
Total population/p.c.										
Alpha = 2.0								.14	-2.38*	-4.13*
R^2	.25*	.19*	.33*	.26*	.24*	.19*	.17	.21*	.81*	.79*
F	4.58	3.41*	4.65*	4.93*	3.27*	3.44*	2.34	3.83*	27.84*	24.61*
Standardized s.e.	.85	.88	.79	.84	.84	.88	.88	.87	.41	.43

*Significance = .05.

131

statistical explanation for its violent crime rate, its property crime rate is better understood in terms of the demographic composition of surrounding neighborhoods. Potentials of total population, teenage population, and poor families are computed with various distance-decay exponents. Neighborhood crime rates are most highly correlated with potentials with the highest distance-decay exponents. This suggests that journey to crime is highly sensitive to distance. When a neighborhood's wealth, local proportion of poor, and poverty potential are included in a multiple regression, variations in both property crime and violent crime rates are highly sensitive to variations in poverty potential.

These results provide credence to the hypothesis that changes in metropolitan structure have contributed to both the suburbanization of crime and its democratization. Improvements in intrametropolitan mobility and the suburbanization of the poor have increased the chances of victimization of the middle class.

Models of ecological succession (Taeuber and Taeuber, 1965; Schelling, 1972; Clotfelter, 1975) identify the conditions under which the entry of a lower-status group into a neighborhood can result in an abandonment of a neighborhood by the higher-status group and its "tipping" to lower status. In these models, the presence of lower-status families on a block or lower-status children in the neighborhood school inflicts external diseconomies on the higher-status families. The present study indicates that externalities may extend far beyond the neighborhood block or school boundaries. The crime rate in a neighborhood can rise as a result of the entry of lower-status families in a neighborhood several miles away.

Previous research (Katzman, 1980) indicates that higher-status families are especially likely to avoid moving into high-crime neighborhoods. As the crime rate in a high-status neighborhhood rises, higher-status families are less likely to replace themselves in the normal turnover in the housing market than to be replaced by lower-status families. The abandonment of the neighborhood by a few higher-status families results in the neighborhood further declining in status. The crime rate rises further because the ratio of local poor and "poverty potential" to higher-status residents rises. This makes the neighborhood even less attractive to higher-status families who are considering moving in. Thus, the fabric of the neighborhood unravels.

NOTES

1. Casual observation of cities and towns in semifeudal circumstances indicates that the degree of residential proximity of upper- and lower-status groups is high, epitomized by the live-in servants' quarters in nineteenth-century Southern cities. Gans (1967) suggests that "residential segregation ... reflects the breakdown of rigid class systems in which low-status people 'know their place' and which made residential segregation unnecessary." Modern American class boundaries are vague, however, and even public discussion of class differences has the aura of taboo. This does not mean that Americans are unaware of differences in behavioral norms among class subcultures or that they are not perceived as important. There are simply no recognized legitimate structures on interclass social relations. Instead, space serves the function of reducing interclass relations outside of the job context, where status and authority are much more clearly defined.

2. The flattening of land value and population density gradients in American cities is consistent with the hypothesis of decreasing friction of distance. See, for example, Mills (1971: 3).

REFERENCES

BOGGS, S. (1966) "Urban crime patterns." American Sociological Review 30: 899-908.

CAPONE, D. L. and W. W. NICHOLS, Jr. (1975) "Crime and distance: an analysis of offender behavior in space." Proceedings of the American Association of Geographers 7: 45-49.

CHAPMAN, J., W. Z. HIRSCH, and S. SONENBLUM (1975) "A police service production function." Public Finance 30: 197-215.

CLOTFELTER, C. T. (1978) "Public security and private safety." Journal of Urban Economics 5 (July): 388-402.

——— (1977) "Urban crime and household protective measures." Review of Economics and Statistics 59 (November): 499-503.

——— (1975) "School desegregation, 'tipping,' and private school enrollment." Journal of Human Resources 11 (December): 28-50.

GANS, H. J. (1967) The Levittowners. New York: Random House.

GEORGES, D. E. (1978) The Geography of Crime and Violence. Resource Papers for College Geography, No. 78-1. American Association of Geographers.

_____and K. KIRKSEY (1977) "Violent crime perpetrated against the elderly in the city of Dallas during the year 1975." Journal of Environmental Systems 7: 203-228.

HAKIM, S., A. OVADIA, and J. WEINBLATT (1978) "Crime attraction and deterrence in small communities: theory and results." International Regional Science Review 3: 153-163.

HAKIM, S., A. OVADIA, E. SAGI, and J. WEINBLATT (1979) "Interjurisdictional spillover of crime and police expenditures." Land Economics 55, 2: 200-212.

HARRIES, K. D. (1974) The Geography of Crime and Justice. New York: McGraw-Hill.

HOCH, I. (1972) "Income and city size." Urban Studies 9: 299-328.

ISARD, W. (1960) Methods of Regional Analysis. Cambridge: MIT Press.

KAIN, J. F. (1969) "Introduction," in J. F. Kain (ed.) Race and Poverty: The Economics of Discrimination. Englewood Cliffs, NJ: Prentice-Hall.

KATZMAN, M. T. (1980) "The contribution of crime to urban decline." Urban Studies 17 (October): 277-286.

_____(1977) "The influence of transportation improvements on interregional trade in Brazil." Transportation 6 (December): 393-408.

_____(1968) "Economics of defense against crime in the streets." Land Economics 44 (November): 331-340.

_____with H. CHILDS (1979) "Black flight: the middle class black reaction to school integration and metropolitan change." University of Texas—Dallas. (unpublished)

KOMESAR, N. K. (1973) "A theoretical and empirical study of victims of crime." Journal of Legal Studies 2 (June): 301-321.

MILLS, E. (1971) Studies in the Structure of the Urban Economy. Baltimore: Johns Hopkins Press.

RENGERT, G. (1979) "Equity considerations in police patrol allocations," in J. W. Frazier and B. J. Epstein (eds.) Applied Geography Conferences: Volume 2. Binghampton: SUNY.

_____(1977) "Burglary in Philadelphia: a critique on an opportunity structure model." Presented at the meeting of the Association of American Geographers, April.

SCHELLING, T. C. (1972) "Neighborhood tipping," pp. 157-184 in A. H. Pascal (ed.) Racial Discrimination in Economic Life. Lexington, MA: D. C. Heath.

SMITH, T. S. (1976) "Inverse distance variations for the flow of crime in urban areas." Social Forces 56: 802-815.

TAEUBER, K. and A. TAEUBER (1965) Negroes in Cities. Chicago: Aldine.

TURNER, S. (1969) "Delinquency and distance," pp. 11-26 in T. Sellin and M. E. Wolfgang (eds.) Delinquency: Selected Studies. New York: John Wiley.

WEICHER, J. C. (1971) "The allocation of police protection by income class." Urban Studies 8 (October): 207-220.

Daryl A. Hellman
Northeastern University

9

CRIMINAL MOBILITY AND POLICY RECOMMENDATIONS

Criminal spatial mobility can be viewed within an economic framework as a characteristic of the criminal production process which creates a potential source of externalities, or spillovers, among communities. To the extent that offenders (producers) are mobile among jurisdictions, they will seek those production locations that yield the highest net expected returns to criminal activity. Thus, various characteristics of one community vis-à-vis another, for example, its provision of police services, can affect the economic well-being of nearby communities by affecting the location decision of area (metropolitan) criminals.

Some portion of this potential for criminal mobility to create externalities has been examined previously. Mehay (1977) demonstrates and empirically tests the criminal spillover effects of differential per capital police inputs across communities in a single-equation model of crime service functions. Hakim et al. (1979) extend the analysis to examine the simultaneous relationship between crime and police expenditures in a spillover context and empirically test their model. Their results suggest that spillovers of both crime and police expenditures exist. Fabrikant (1980) examines spillovers of juvenile offenders and finds that spillovers, while small, depend, as expected, on the net returns to criminal activity. Fabrikant's data included origin and destination of offender, thus permitting better specification of the problem. The purpose of this chapter is to build on this earlier work and to combine it with other research on models of crime, law enforcement, and the public sector to examine more fully the sources of externalities among communities and to assess the associated policy implications. Specifically, the chapter will expand consideration of community spillovers due to criminal mobility by posing the Mehay argument within the context of a simultaneous equation model of crime, law enforcement, and the public sector to emphasize the public policy issues involved.

The first section contains a summary of the Mehay single-equation model. In the second section, criminal spatial mobility is examined within the framework of a more complete simultaneous systems approach. The following section contains a discussion of the policy implications of the externalities generated by criminal mobility viewed within the simultaneous systems context. The final section contains conclusions.

THE MEHAY MODEL

Mehay begins by specifying a production function for crime-deterrent police services with production externalities across jurisdictions:[1]

$$0_i = 0(I_i, I_j, z_i, T) \qquad [1]$$

where 0_i = crime rate in community i (output);
I_i = crime-deterrent police inputs in i;
I_j = crime-deterrent police inputs in j;
z_i = environmental factors in community i which affect police productivity; and
T = crime-control technology.

It is the I_j term which is included to account for the spillover effect. A change in police inputs in any neighboring community j, *ceteris paribus,* affects the productivity of police in community i in deterring crime, that is, it affects the crime rate in community i. Other things being equal, producers of criminal activity will relocate toward community i in response to the increase in relative costs of production (expected punishment costs) in community j. In order to maintain its crime level, community i would therefore have to increase its expenditure on crime-deterrent police and increase police inputs.

Mehay (1977: 1353) assumes that the spillover effect is "unidirectional and non-reciprocal, caused by a divergence from an initial equilibrium position between input levels in the two adjacent communities." Thus, as community i increases police inputs, there is no spillover effect back on j unless i were to overadjust. Were this not the case, crime would be continuously shifting across boundaries in response to each input change.

An additional assumption required is that prior to the increase in police inputs in j there are excess profits being earned by the criminal industry in both communities. Were this not the case, the increase in expected punishment costs in j would not only reduce crime in j, but would also reduce total crime in the area, since some criminals would leave the industry; there would be no room for relocation in community i. It is not only the relative profitability of crime across communities that is important, but also the profitability of crime relative to legal income-producing activities. When illegal earnings net of costs approach legal alternatives, rational criminals leave the illegal sector. Thus crime displacement can occur only when excess profits are being earned.[2] One feature of the simultaneous system approach, as we shall see, is inclusion of separate supply of crime and law enforcement production functions. This has the advantage, among others, of clarifying the criminal location decision and, therefore, the crime displacement issue.

The equation used by Mehay for empirical testing of the spillover effect is:

$$0_i = \frac{(d_{PL}, p_i, Pov_i, NW_i, RS_i)}{P} \qquad [2]$$

where O_i = crime rate in community i ;

$\dfrac{d_{PL}}{P}$ = difference between police patrol persons per capita in community i and the average in all cities (j) adjacent to i;[3]

P_i = clearance rate in i;

Pov_i = percentage of families in i below the poverty line;

NW_i = percentage of the population in i nonwhite;

M_i = percentage of males $\geqslant$ 14 years old in i married; and

RS_i = taxable retail sales in i per 1,000 population.

It is the first variable of equation 2 which is included to test the spillover effect. It is expected that, other things equal, an increase in the police input differential between i and its neighbors will increase the crime rate in i (given that the police input increases in neighboring cities).

The rest of the variables included in equation 2 are fairly typical and require no explanation here. They are the empirical counterparts to z, environmental factors in i, in equation 1. One point, however, should be made. In equation 2 the only comparison between i and j assumed to be relevant in the criminal decision is the difference in visible patrol per capita. Yet, the rational criminal location decision is based on a comparison of net returns to crime in various communities among which he or she is mobile. Thus, not only cost differences, but differences in the gains from criminal acts should be included, that is, the RS variable should be measured relative to adjacent communities. Again, formulation of the spillover problem within a simultaneous system with a separate supply of offenses function will clarify this point.

Mehay tests his model using 46 cities in the Los Angeles metropolitan area. Separate equations are tested for crimes against property and crimes against persons, which exhibit different results. In the property crime equation the police input differential is positive and significant, while in the violent crime equation the same variable is statistically insignificant. Thus, the spillover effect is supported for those kinds of crimes perhaps most subject to police deterrence. The relative magnitude, however, of the estimated spillover effect is small; the results indicate that a 10 percent increase in the police input differential would lead to a less than 1 percent increase in crimes against property in any one adjacent community.[4] The total effect in the metropolitan area, of course, would depend on the number of neighbors.

A SIMULTANEOUS EQUATION MODEL

We begin with a general simultaneous equation model of urban crime, law enforcement, and the public sector in order to illustrate the primary interactions.[5] This general model is then respecified below, to account for spillovers within an urban area. The model includes a supply of crime function, a law enforcement production function, a police expenditure function, an urban property value function, and, finally, a city revenue function, or budget constraint:

$$O = O (p, f, E, Val, z) \qquad [3]$$
$$p = p (Ct, Cor, E, O) \qquad [4]$$
$$E = E (O, CRev) \qquad [5]$$
$$Val = Val (O, PS, tx, q, s) \qquad [6]$$
$$CRev = CRev (Val, tx, Rev, IGT) \qquad [7]$$

where O = crime rate;
  p = probability of punishment (arrest and conviction);
  f = average length of sentence;
  E = police expenditures;
  Val = property value;
  z = criminogenic environmental factors (such as density, percentage poor, unemployment rate);
  Ct = court input characteristics (such as per capita expenditures on criminal courts, proportion spent on judges);
  Cor = corrections input characteristics (such as expenditures on corrections, percentage of capacity available);

CRev = local public service characteristics (such as school expenditures per pupil);

tx = effective property tax rate;

q = housing and land-use characteristics (such as housing quality, density, land-use mix);

s = socioeconomic characteristics (such as income, age, percentage nonwhite);

Rev = nonproperty local "own" revenue; and

IGT = intergovernmental transfers.

In equation 3, the supply of crime is hypothesized to be a negative function of expected punishment costs as measured by the probability of arrest and conviction, average sentence length, and police expenditures. The latter is included to account for the impact of police expenditures on perceived probabilities of arrest, independent of an impact on actual arrest rates. Val is included in the supply of crime function to measure gains from (property) crime. (Alternative measures would be income level or average retail sales.) The equation is completed by inclusion of various criminogenic environmental factors which directly or indirectly affect the net returns to criminal activity in urban areas. Inclusion of poverty, income, or unemployment variables is done to measure legal returns available, against which illegal returns must be compared. Alternative specifications of the supply of crime function can be found in the literature (see Orsagh, 1970; Sjoquist, 1973; Phillips and Votey, 1975; Ehrlich, 1973; Greenwood and Wadycki, 1973; McPheters and Stronge, 1974; Wilson and Boland, 1978). Equation 3 represents a synthesis of the previous theoretical and empirical work.

Equation 4 is a law enforcement production function with the probability of arrest and conviction as a measure of output. (Alternative specifications are found in Orsagh, 1970; Phillips and Votey, 1975; Ehrlich, 1973; Wilson and Boland, 1978.) In addition to police expenditures, court and corrections input characteristics are included to account for the influence of the various components of the criminal justice system on the deterrence function. Thus the potential influence of larger political districts, such as court districts and the state, on the conviction rate and, therefore, on local crime rates, are recognized. The offense rate is included in equation 4 as a workload proxy. Other things equal, as the number of offenses increases, the arrest and conviction rate has to drop.

Police expenditures, equation 5, are hypothesized to be a positive function of the crime rate, a demand factor, and of city revenues, a supply constraint. Similar specifications of the police expenditures function are found in Greenwood and Wadycki (1973) and McPheters and Stronge (1974). Ehrlich (1973) specifies a partial adjustment process by the introduction of a distributed lag function.

Equation 6 is a city property value function. Aggregate property values are hypothesized to be a negative function of the crime rate, since crime affects the utility (profitability) of property in an area. Property values also depend on the public service package and the effective tax rate, both of which may be capitalized into values. Finally, property values depend on various housing quality and land-use characteristics, as well as socioeconomic characteristics of the population which affect the demand for property. Hellman and Naroff (1979) present theoretical and empirical justification for this type of property value equation. Gray and Joelson (1979) use a similar form in an empirically oriented single-equation model. Mehay (1978) uses a similar equation to test the impact of an intergovernmental contract police services plan on property values. Mehay addresses the tax/public services capitalization issue.

The final equation of the model, 7, is a city revenue function. By definition, city (town) revenues depend on "own" source revenues and intergovernmental transfers. The former depend primarily on the value of property and the effective property tax rate, since the property tax is the major source of local revenues. To correct for additional own sources of revenue, such as a local sales or income tax, or user charges, the variable Rev is included.

This model has several advantages: (1) it separates the supply of crime function from the law enforcement production function, clarifying the relationships and avoiding well-known problems involved in using a production function with crime as an output measure; (2) it includes the impact of crime on property values, tax revenues, and, therefore, police expenditures; (3) it recognizes the potential importance of intergovernmental transfers to local expenditures; and (4) it identifies the possible constraints imposed by characteristics of the courts or corrections on the productivity of local police. Nevertheless, when used to describe the interactions among criminal activity, law enforcement, and the public sector within metropolitan areas, the model must be adjusted to incorporate the potential for spatial mobility, not only of criminals, but of property users and customers of commercial establishments.

Within a metropolitan context, appropriate specification of the model becomes:

$$O_i = O(d_p, d_f, d_E, d_{Val}, z_i) \qquad [8]$$

$$p_i = p(Ct_i, Cor_i, E_i, O_i) \qquad [9]$$

$$E_i = E(O_i, CRev_i) \qquad [10]$$

$$Val_i = Val(d_o, d_{PS}, d_{tx}, q_i, s_i) \qquad [11]$$

$$CRev_i = CRev(Val_i, tx_i, Rev_i, IGT_i) \qquad [12]$$

$$\text{where } d_x = \frac{\sum\limits_{j=1}^{n} X_j}{n} - X_i.^6$$

In the respecified model, the supply of offenses and property value equations are altered to account for spatial mobility and, thus, spillovers. In the supply of offenses equation, 8, measures of expected punishment cost, p, f, and E, are replaced by comparative measures across communities, d_p, d_f, d_E.[7] In addition, the relative gain from crime across communities is included, d_{Val}. Thus the spatial mobility of the criminal is recognized.

In the property equation, 11, relative crime rates, public service packages, and tax rates (d_o, d_{PS}, d_{tx}) replace their absolute levels in order to recognize the spatial mobility of property users (buyers) and shoppers. A relatively high crime rate in a community, measured by d_o, can affect property values directly by decreasing the utility derived from owning or renting residential property, thus reducing demand, and indirectly by discouraging shoppers, reducing sales and profitability of commercial establishments, thus reducing commercial property values. Similarly, the relative quality of public services other than crime control, d_{PS}, and relative effective tax rates, d_{tx}, affect the locational choice of households, as well as other land users.

The remaining equations in the model are unaffected. However, in equation 9, the measures of court and corrections inputs, Ct and Cor, may become constant over a metropolitan area, and therefore drop out of the equation. The probability of punishment in any particular community then depends only on the community's own expenditures on police and on its crime rate, or workload.

POLICY IMPLICATIONS

The full policy implications of criminal spatial mobility can now be addressed. Again, we examine the impact of an increase in police expenditures in community j caused by a divergence from an initial equilibrium position between input levels in j and adjacent community i. This increase in expenditure will, other things being equal, cause the crime rate in i to increase, because both d_p and d_E increase. If criminals are mobile, and given excess profits in the criminal industry, criminals will relocate in i as expected punishments costs in j increase relative to i. This is the first-round effect of the increased expenditure in j.

The increase in the crime rate in i, ΔO_i, triggers a number of reactions in i. From equation 9 we see that, other things equal, an increase in O_i will cause p_i to decrease, leading to still further increases in i's crime rate. However, other things will not remain equal, since the increase in crime will also cause increased expenditures on police in i (equation 10) which act to increase p_i and decrease O_i, both directly and indirectly, offsetting at least some of the first-round impact. Whether the crime rate in i experiences a net increase or decrease depends on: (1) the magnitude of the initial spill-over effect; (2) the relative responsiveness of the probability of punishment in i to increases in expenditures, on the one hand, and changes in the crime rate on the other; (3) the responsiveness of the crime rate to changes in expected punishment costs; and (4) the magnitude of the increase in police expenditures in i which, in part, depends on the responsiveness of police expenditures to changes in the community crime rate.

It is at this point that the impact of crime on property values and city (town) revenues becomes important. From equation 11 we see that an increase in i's crime rate relative to other communities will decrease property values in i. This will eventually cause local public revenues in i to drop (equation 12) as reduced values are reflected in reduced assessments. Reduced public revenues in turn will cause police expenditures to be reduced (equation 10). Thus, because of the impact of crime on property values and tax loss, the increase in police expenditures, expected in response to an increase in the crime rate, will be less than expected because of a tightened local budget constraint. In the absence of increased intergovernmental transfers to restore the fiscal position of the community, community i may not be able to restore crime to its previous level, regardless of a strong taste for law enforcement, that is, in spite of a large positive elasticity of police expenditures with respect to the crime rate. While the constraint imposed by decreased property values may not be realized immediately, it will nevertheless have an impact. It is true that the reduction in property values in i relative to neighboring communities would serve to reduce property crimes (equation 8). However, if an alternative measure of gains in the supply of crime function were a better indicator of gains, then the mitigating impact would disappear.

Estimates of the parameters of the model outlined would permit determination and comparison of the magnitudes of the various impacts. However, our emphasis here is on the "property value effect." A measure of the importance of this effect is provided by coefficients estimated using Boston census tracts as the units of observation (Naroff et al., 1980). Because of the data base used, the five-equation model simplifies to two: a supply of crime function and a property value function. Three-stage least squares estimates of the coefficients indicate that the elasticity of property value with respect to crime is −1.67 (significant at the 99 percent level).[8] Thus, a 1 percent increase in the crime rate in a community (perhaps caused by spillovers) would lead to a 1.67 percent decrease in the community's "own" revenues. In the absence of compensating intergovernmental transfers, this means a 1.67 percent decrease in the community's budget and expenditures.[9]

How much this reduced budget means for police expenditures depends on the income elasticity of police expenditures. Previous studies have found positive and significant impacts on the revenue constraint on police expenditures (Greenwood and Wadycki, 1973; McPheters and Stronge, 1974), although the estimated impacts are small (for example, Greenwood and Wadycki's estimated elasticity of police expenditures with respect to tax base is 0.18). It is possible that more recent estimates would show greater sensitivity, especially because of the increasing lack of flexibility in many local budgets due to certain "fixed" obligations, such as pensions and debt service.[10]

It is interesting to apply the parameter estimate for the city of Boston. In 1976, a 1 percent increase in the crime rate would have reduced city revenues by $6.4 million. By comparison, the police budget for that year was $47.3 million. Thus the revenue reduction is a substantial proportion of "nonfixed" expenditures, which include police; police and fire protection are typically the largest components, after education (in Massachusetts, the autonomy of local school committees makes educational expenditures much less vulnerable to cuts than other expenditure categories). Under these circumstances it is difficult to believe that a $6.4 million revenue cut would not have a measurable impact on city police expenditures (other than pension payments).[11]

Clearly, the revenue reduction has lead to decreased provision of some services, whether police protection or something else. If the remainder of the public service package is sacrificed so that police protection can be maintained, property values in the community will be reduced as the reduction in public services relative to neighboring communities becomes capitalized in lower property values. If property values are more sensitive to the lack of police protection (that is, the crime rate) than to the lack of other public services, then it would make sense for the community to adjust in this manner. The elasticities of property value with respect to crime and with respect to the rest of the public service package would have to be compared.[12]

Regardless of the choice made, the community is worse off. Thus, if the initial increase in crime in the community is the result of crime spillovers, decisions made by neighboring communities lead to welfare losses in the community. These losses are not only in the form of direct losses from increased crime, but also in the form of reduced property values and reduced ability to finance public services, including crime control. Use of intergovernmental transfer payments may be appropriate to compensate the community for losses.[13]

In the absence of compensating intergovernmental transfers, an alternative solution is police agency consolidation, which can be achieved in a variety of ways, such as intergovernmental contracting, or, more generally, formation of metropolitan-wide governments. Alleged benefits of consolidation include improved efficiency and equity via elimination of the spillover problem, and potential advantages of economies of scale. On the other hand, "local control" and possibilities for product differentiation are sacrificed. In sum, it is not clear that consolidation leads to improved provision of police services (Mehay, 1978). Interestingly enough, a recent study states that since 1970, more than 1,000 communities have studied the feasibility of police consolidation, and that currently an estimated 500 communities are engaged in operational consolidation (Koepsell and Girard, 1979).

This movement toward consolidation, however, is not evidence that actual, or even perceived, spillover problems exist. The movement could be explained entirely by actual or perceived economies of scale. Nor is it evidence that the spillover problem is being solved. In fact, most of the police consolidations serve areas of less than 25,000 people, suggesting that the consolidation movement is greatest in non-metropolitan and rural areas, areas in which the spillover problem would be expected to be least important. In 1973, the National Advisory Commission on Criminal Justice Standards and Goals recommended police consolidation, but in cases where departments had less than ten full-time sworn officers (Koepsell and Girard, 1979: 7). Thus the consolidation movement is most likely explained more by cost advantages, whether perceived or actual, than spillover effects, and, if spillovers exist in the more densely settled and mobile metropolitan areas, they are not being removed by consolidation in these areas.

CONCLUSIONS

At this point there are few firm conclusions that can be drawn. First, it is not clear that the magnitude of the criminal spillover effect is large. The empirical results to date suggest that if spillovers exist, they are relatively small. In addition, there are theoretical reasons for believing that crime spillovers may be insignificant. To the extent that the criminal industry is competitive and entrance into the industry is not restricted, excess profits should not persist and criminal spillovers should be negligible. If, however, the spillover effect is significant, it has the additional harmful effect on neighboring communities of reducing their tax bases and abilities to finance crime control. This can serve to aggravate the spillover problem. Compensating intergovernmental transfer payments may be warranted.

Police agency consolidation is an alternative solution. However, agency consolidation, while it can solve the spillover problem, may lead to increased costs of operation (if there are diseconomies of scale) and loss of local control. As of yet the evidence on the advantages or disadvantages of scale for police departments is not conclusive. Thus, it may be a mistake to consolidate departments to solve an alleged spillover problem, particularly if the benefits of economies of scale are not well documented. Intergovernmental transfers would be a preferred alternative.

Finally, it should be noted that the spillover effect hinges on the relative profitability of crime in different locations. According to the argument, increases in police expenditures and inputs in one community are expected to increase expected punishment costs in that community and, therefore, export crime. Even if this potential for spillovers exists, however, it must be recognized that the police are just part of the criminal justice system and, therefore, just part of the determination of expected punishment costs. Activities in the other components of the criminal justice system may be equally, or more important. If these components of the system have service areas which are metropolitan-wide or larger, then the spillover impact of differential police expenditures may be mitigated.

NOTES

1. Equations are presented with revised symbols for comparability.

2. Unless criminals are risk-preferrers. For a discussion of this issue, see Ehrlich (1973).

3.

$$\frac{d_{PL}}{P} = \frac{\sum\limits_{j=1}^{n} \dfrac{PL_j}{P_j}}{n} - \frac{PL_i}{P_i}$$

4. While the smallness of the spillover effect measured by Mehay may be due to the particular manner in which he formulates the problem, it could be argued that a small effect is expected to the extent that the industry is competitive and excess profits are eliminated by entry into the industry.

5. This model is an adaptation of the one contained in Hellman and Naroff (1980). Earlier versions are contained in Hellman and Naroff (1979) and Naroff et al. (1980). Hellman and Naroff (1980) present a review and critique of fourteen other related model-building efforts.

6. This is but one way of measuring d_x which follows the Mehay specifications. A ratio of X_i to the average value in adjacent communities would avoid any restrictions on the value of the coefficient of d_x. In addition, the community aver-

age could be calculated by weighting community values differently, for example, by relative magnitude of common borders, or distance between community centers i and j.

7. Average sentence length, f, may not vary across communities if charged offenders from all communities have access to the same courts.

8. In the supply of crime function, the coefficient of property values is negative and significant at the 92.5 percent level.

9. The community could offset decreases in property value assessments by increases in the property tax rate or rate of other own taxes or charges. This, however, would mean an increase in the relative tax position of the community vis-à-vis its neighbors, and, from equation 11, additional reductions in property value.

10. In Massachusetts, these fixed obligations currently represent from 20 to 40 percent of a municipality's budget.

11. Even larger relative impacts are found by Gray and Joelson (1979). In a single-equation model of the impact of crime on property values in Minneapolis, they estimate that, in 1975, crime generated a total estimated tax revenue loss of about $13 million, compared with a city criminal justice system budget of $19 million.

12. A third alternative is to increase taxes, so a comparison with the elasticity of property value with respect to taxes is also relevant. See note 9. Mehay (1978) finds that property values are more sensitive to service quality than tax rates.

13. Even if the increase in crime is not due to spillovers, intergovernmental transfers may be required if, because of the property value effect, local governments' expenditures on crime control (or other public services) is less than that deemed appropriate from a national (state) perspective.

REFERENCES

ALLISON, J. P. (1972) "Economic factors and the rate of crime." Land Economics (May): 193-196.

BECKER, G. S. (1968) "Crime and punishment: an economic approach." Journal of Political Economy (March/April): 169-217.

BLUMSTEIN, A. and R. LARSON (1969) "Models of a total criminal justice system." Operations Research: 199-231.

EHRLICH, I. (1973) "Participation in illegitimate activities: a theoretical and empirical investigation." Journal of Political Economy (May/June): 521-564.

FABRIKANT, R. (1980) "Interjurisdictional spillovers of urban police services: comment." Southern Economic Journal (January): 955-961.

GRAY, C. M. and M. R. JOELSON (1979) "Neighborhood crime and the demand for central city housing," pp. 47-59 in C. M. Gray (ed.) The Costs of Crime. Beverly Hills, CA: Sage.

GREENWOOD, M. J. and W. J. WADYCKI (1973) "Crime rates and public expenditure for police protection: their interaction." Review of Social Economy (October): 138-151.

HAKIM, S., A. OVADIA, E. SAGI, and J. WEINBLATT (1979) "Interjurisdictional spillover of crime and police expenditure." Land Economics (May): 200-213.

HARRIS, J. R. (1970) "On the economics of law and order." Journal of Political Economy (January/February): 165-174.

HELLMAN, D. and J. NAROFF (1980) The Urban Public Sector and Urban Crime: A Simultaneous System Approach. Washington, DC: National Institute of Justice.

_____ (1979) "The impact of crime on urban residential property values." Urban Studies (February): 105-112.

KATZMAN, M. T. (1968) "The economics of defense against crime in the streets." Land Economics (November): 431-440.

KOEPSELL, T. W. and C. M. GIRARD (1979) Small Police Agency Consolidation: Suggested Approaches. Washington, DC: Office of Development, Testing and Dissemination, National Institute of Law Enforcement and Criminal Justice.

McPHETERS, L. R. and W. B. STRONGE (1974) "Law enforcement expenditures and urban crime." National Tax Journal (December): 633-643.

MEHAY, S. L. (1978) "Governmental structure and performance: the effects of the Lakewood Plan on property value." Public Finance Quarterly (July): 311-325.

_____ (1977) "Interjurisdictional spillovers of urban police services." Southern Economic Journal (January): 1352-1359.

NAROFF, J., D. HELLMAN, and D. SKINNER (1980) "Estimates of the impact of crime on property values: the Boston experience." Growth and Change (October): 24-30.

ORSAGH, T. J. (1970) "The determinants of major crime in California in 1960." Presented at the Western Economic Association meetings, University of California—Davis, August.

PHILLIPS, L. (1977) "Factor demands in the provision of public safety." Center for the Econometric Studies of Crime and the Criminal Justice System, Hoover Institution, Stanford University. (unpublished)

PHILLIPS, L. and H. L. VOTEY, J. (1975) "Crime control in California." Journal of Legal Studies (June): 327-349.

_____ (1972) "An economic analysis of the deterrent effect of law enforcement on criminal activity." Journal of Criminal Law, Criminology, and Police Science (September): 330-342.

_____ and D. MAXWELL (1972) "Crime, youth, and the labor market: an econometric study." Journal of Political Economy (May/June): 491-503.

PRESSMAN, I. and A. CAROL (1971) "Crime as a diseconomy of scale." Review of Social Economy (September): 227-236.

SJOQUIST, D. L. (1973) "Property crime and economic behavior: some empirical results." American Economic Review (June): 439-446.

STIGLER, G. (1970) "The optimum enforcement of laws." Journal of Political Economy (May/June): 526-536.

WILSON, J. Q. and B. BOLAND (1978) "The effect of the police on crime." Law and Society Review (Spring): 367-390.

ABOUT THE AUTHORS

RICHARD S. FABRIKANT is Assistant Professor in the Department of Economics, University of Denver.

SIMON HAKIM is Associate Professor in the Department of Economics, Temple University.

DARYL A. HELLMAN is Professor in the Department of Economics and Director of the Center for Urban and Regional Economics Studies, Northeastern University.

MARTIN T. KATZMAN is Professor of Political Economy and Environmental Sciences in the Graduate Program in Environmental Sciences, University of Texas — Dallas.

JOHN P. McIVER is a Researcher in the Workshop in Political Theory and Policy Analysis at Indiana University — Bloomington.

LEE R. McPHETERS is Professor in the Department of Economics, Arizona State University.

STEPHEN L. MEHAY is Associate Professor in the Department of Economics, San Jose State University.

GEORGE F. RENGERT is Associate Professor in the Department of Geography, Temple University.

JOHN A. SORRENTINO, Jr., is Associate Professor in the Department of Economics, Temple University.

URIEL SPIEGEL is a Lecturer in the Department of Economics, Bar-Ilan University, Ramat-Gan, Israel. He is currently a Visiting Lecturer in the Department of Economics, University of Pennsylvania.

WILLIAM B. STRONGE is Associate Professor and Chair of the Department of Economics, Florida Atlantic University. He is currently a visiting faculty member at Boston College.